Est. SCHIFFER PUBLISHING 1974

Inspiring through expert knowledge

e Maine Coast

ɔK,
friend.

e
posal:

nique
Design

Skills
terial
style

Insignia
on

e Learning
Grade

19310
com

com

The Maine Coast

MICHAEL KAHN

SCHIFFER PUBLISHING
4880 Lower Valley Road • Atglen, PA 19310

To my wife, Christine, who crafted this book
And to the people and organizations who
help preserve the Maine coast

INTRODUCTION

I first came to Maine as a young child with my family. We drove eight hours to Kennebunkport, where we rented a cottage on Goose Rocks Beach. My memories of this trip are like blurred photographs, vignettes of a deep, cold, green ocean whose water receded mysteriously twice a day, revealing granite ledges and islands punctuated with spruce and seaweed, crab shells and mud. There were lobster boats tied to docks stacked with traps made of wood. The piers were made of cut granite blocks, dripping with seaweed, and the pilings were crusted with jagged barnacles and mussels. I remember schooners made from trees and rough rope and canvas sails stained with salt and pitch.

These images left me with more questions than answers. Over the next half century, I would paddle, sail, and hike the seemingly infinite coast of Maine, eventually trying to piece together this rugged coastline onto film.

Glacial ice carved through granite rocks, leaving glacial erratics and islands, all of them unique, subtly different from each other. What I later came to realize was that the coast formed the people as well. It shaped the inhabitants and created an independent, creative, practical community that lives and relies on the ocean, land, and wind for their livelihood. I remember an old lobster-boat builder who crafted them from wood. He proudly brought me into his shed and showed me the most beautiful sailboat; it was full keeled and smoothly planked. He said to me, "*I always wanted to build a sailboat*." I asked him if he had drawn plans, and he turned to the bench where there sat a hand-carved model hull; he picked it up with his strong, rough hands and said, "No plans, but I carved this." To this day, I still do not know how he did it, but the ingenuity of "Mainers" is truly astounding.

I feel like I have only begun to scratch the surface and will continue trying to translate the puzzle of the Maine coast onto film. I will always be enchanted by its wild beauty and by the people who live in the midst of, work in, and preserve this rare treasure.

Here on the coast of Maine, when the long streamers of fog drift in from the sea, sounds are hushed and surroundings become unfamiliar. Near at hand the mullein leaves, great woolly blankets, turn to silver as the mist collects upon them. The old lichen-covered apple trees drip small showers when a vagrant wind stirs the branches. In the distance the encircling spruces come and go as the fog lifts or falls. I have had visitors shiver and ask, "How can you live here? It would depress me." But there are others who say nothing, they just fade into the fog along the shore road and come back presently with their checks red, their eyes bright, and their spirits calm and whisper, "How wonderful."

—ROY BARRETTE

I would really rather feel bad in Maine
than feel good anywhere else.

—E. B. WHITE

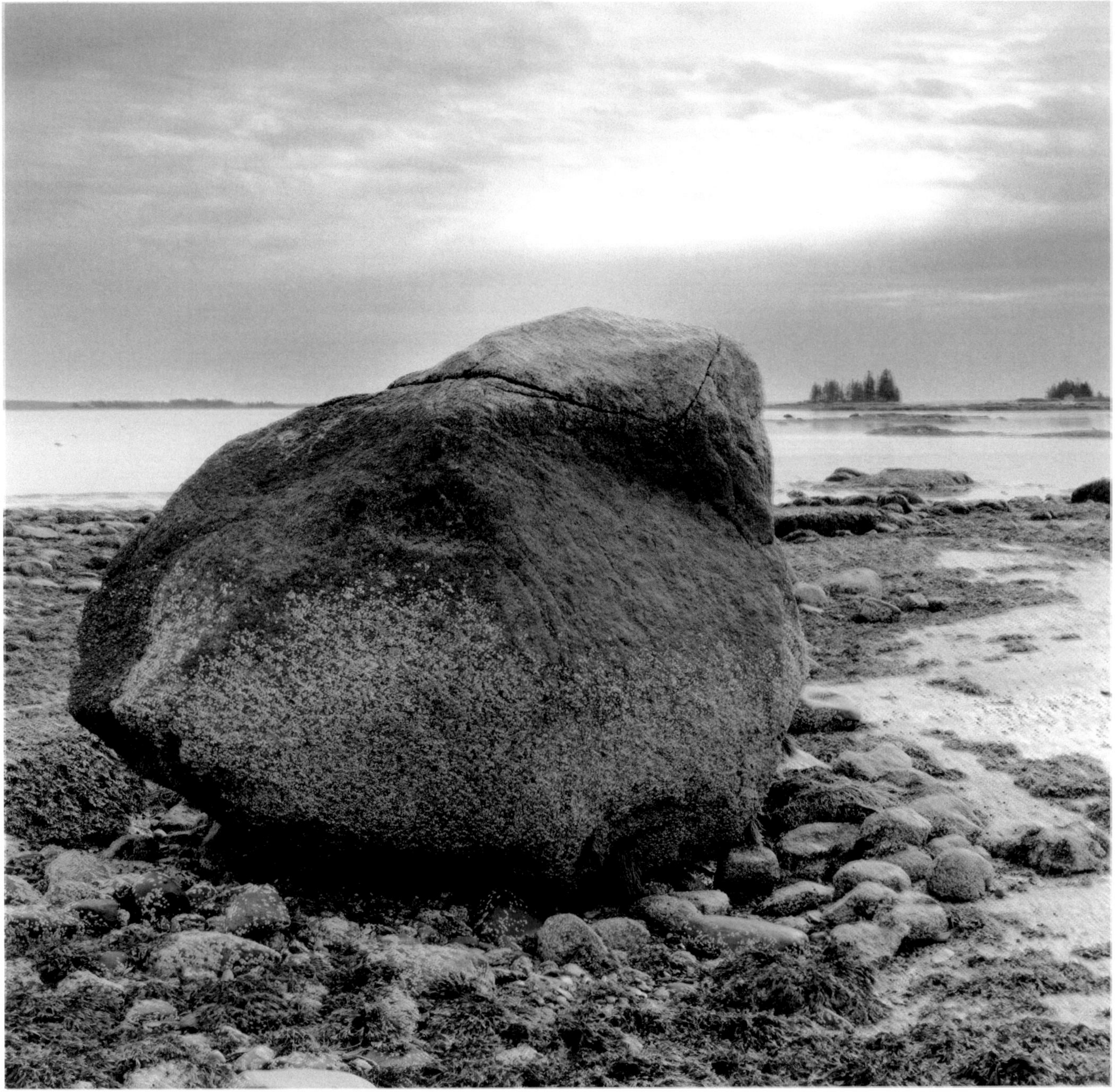

Flye Point, 2021

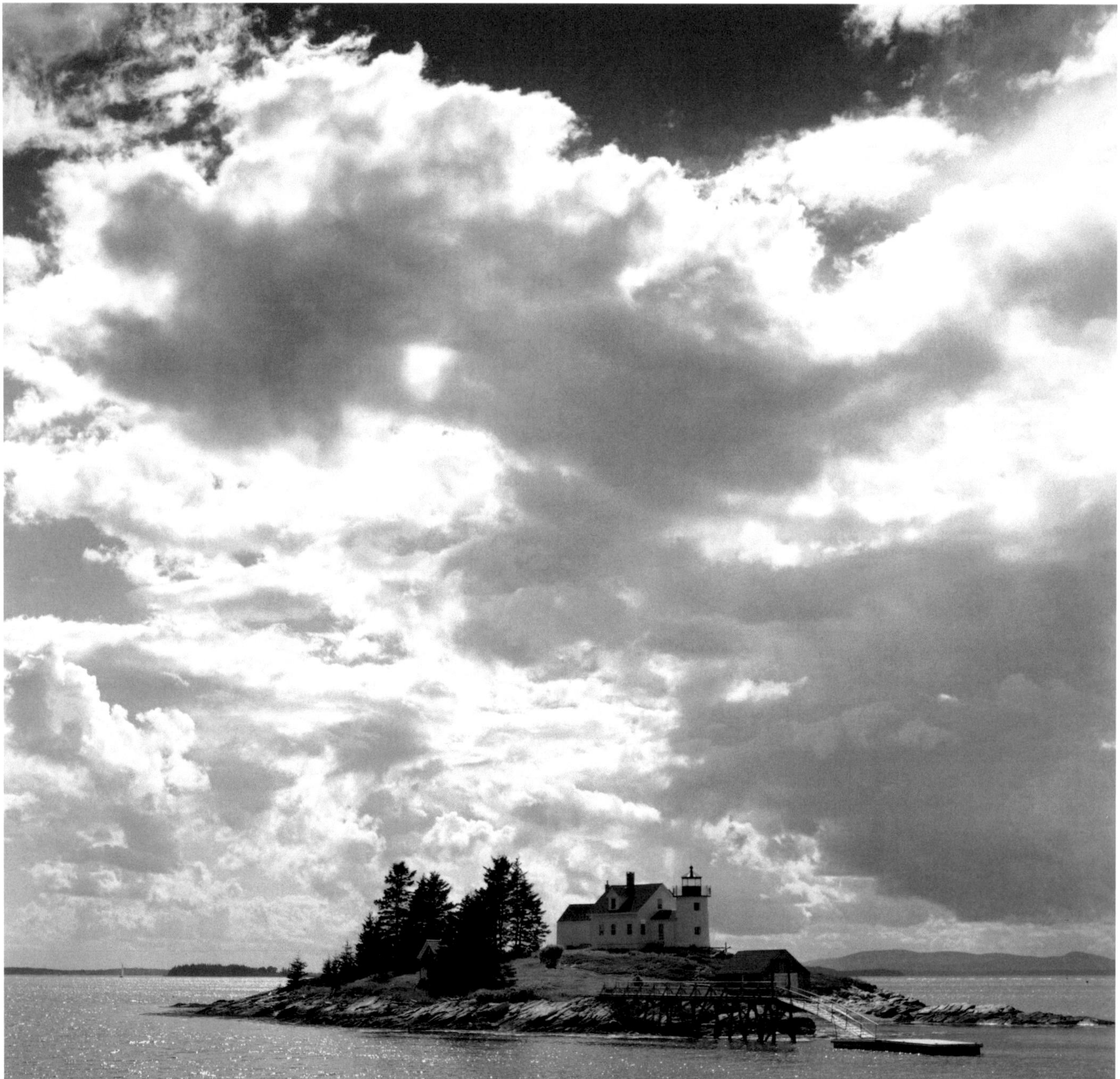

Pumpkin Island Light, 2004

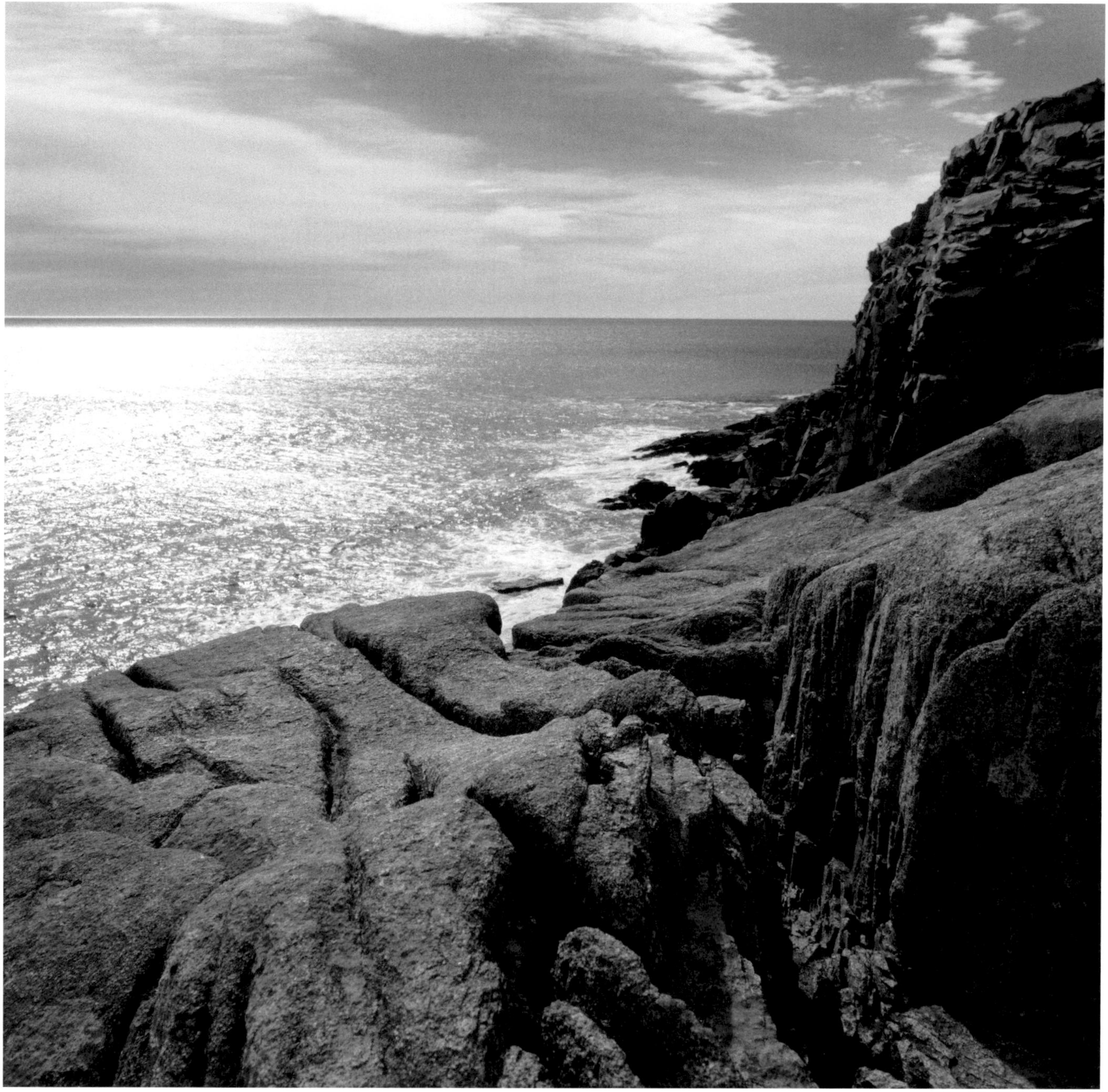

Acadia National Park, 2022

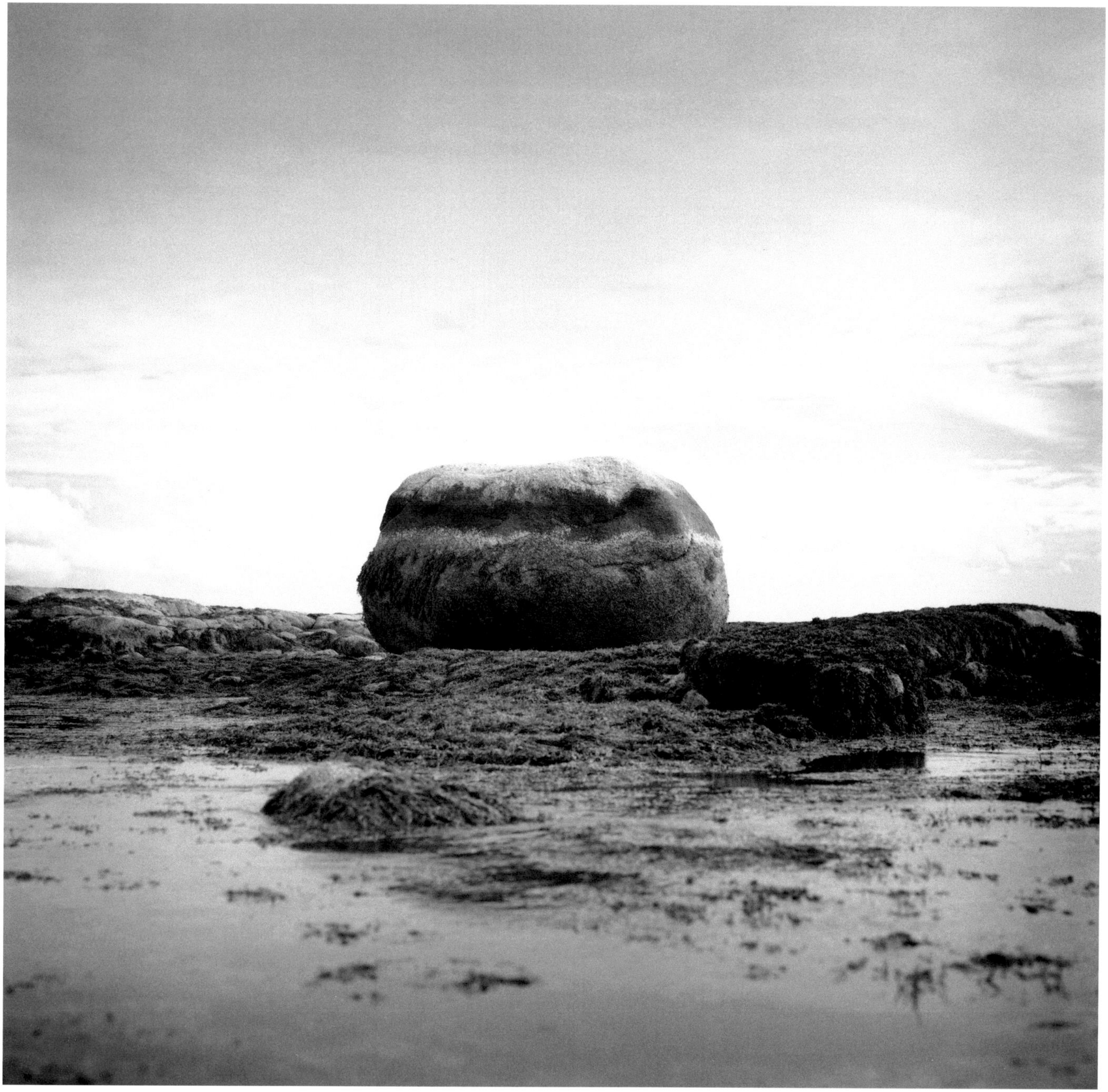

Harbor Island, 2022

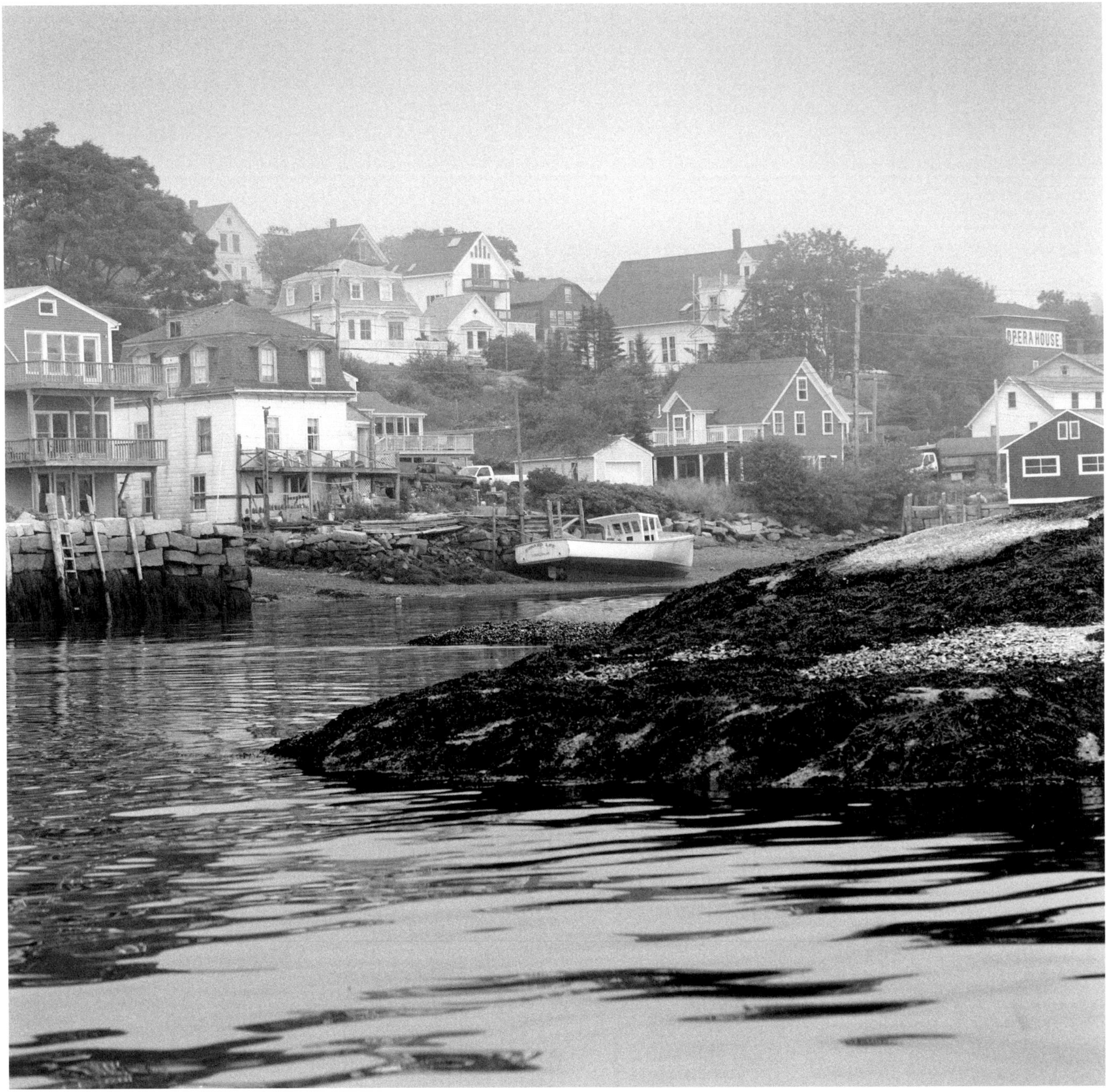

Stonington, 2006

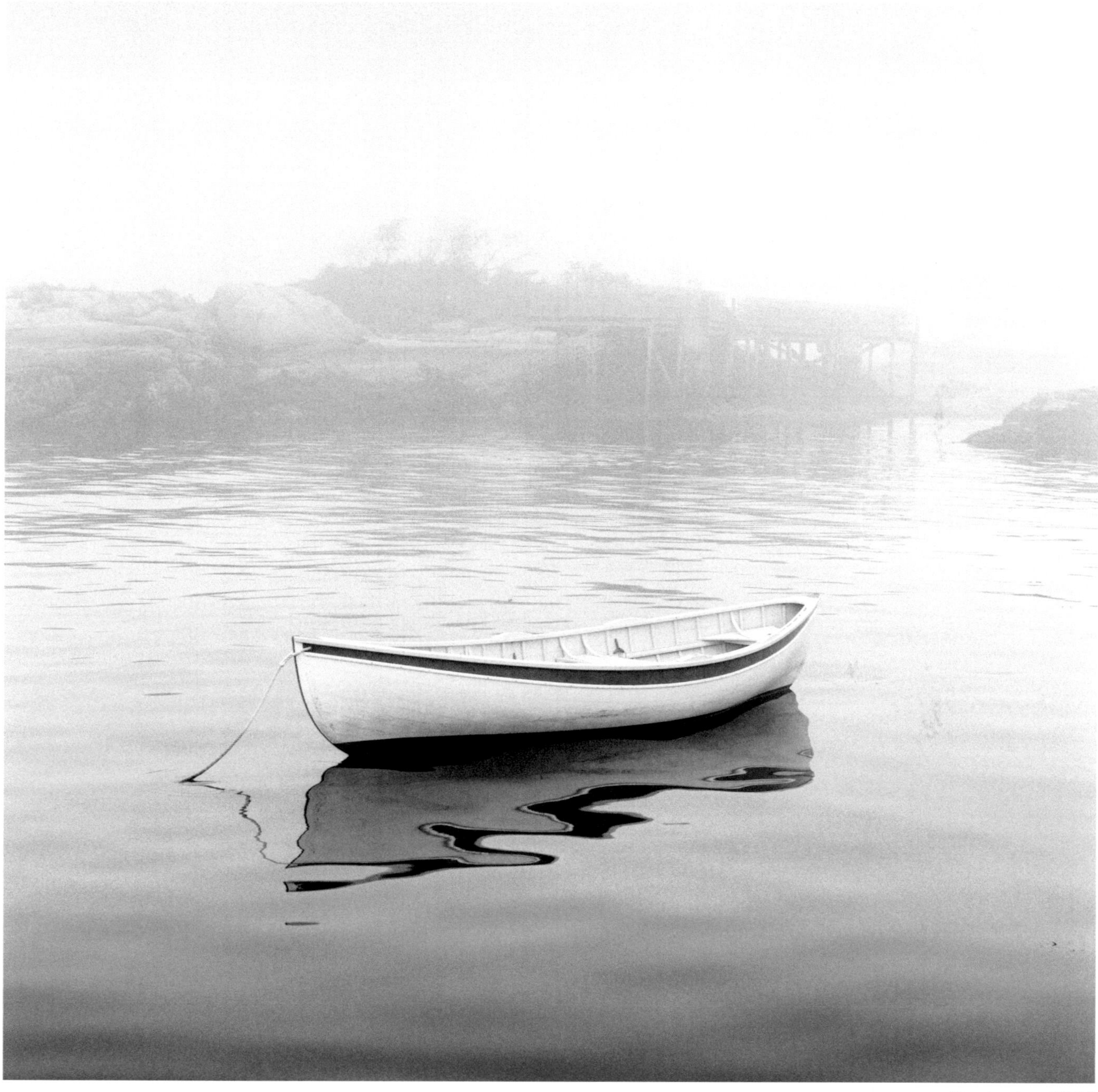

Stonington, 2006

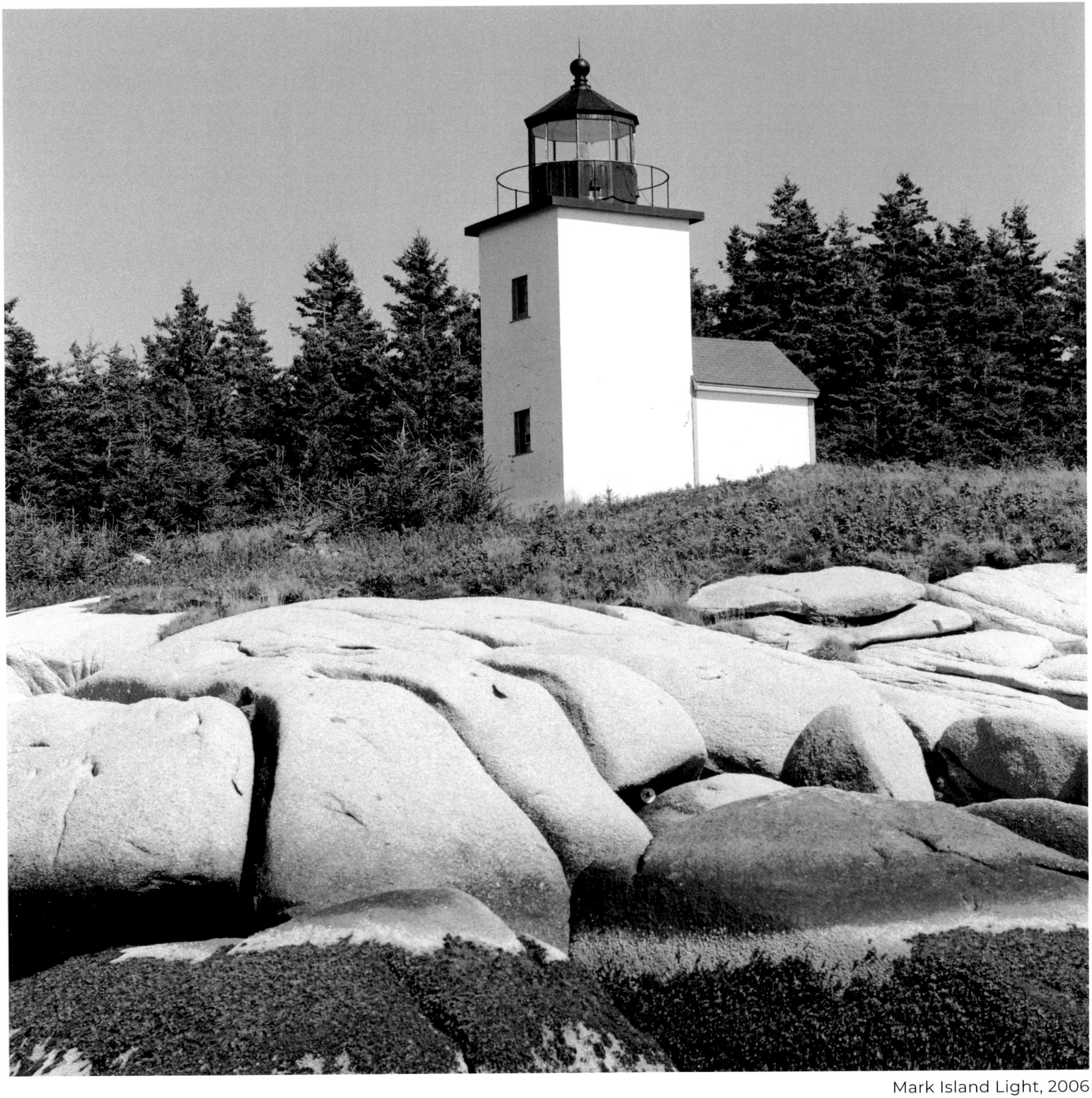

Mark Island Light, 2006

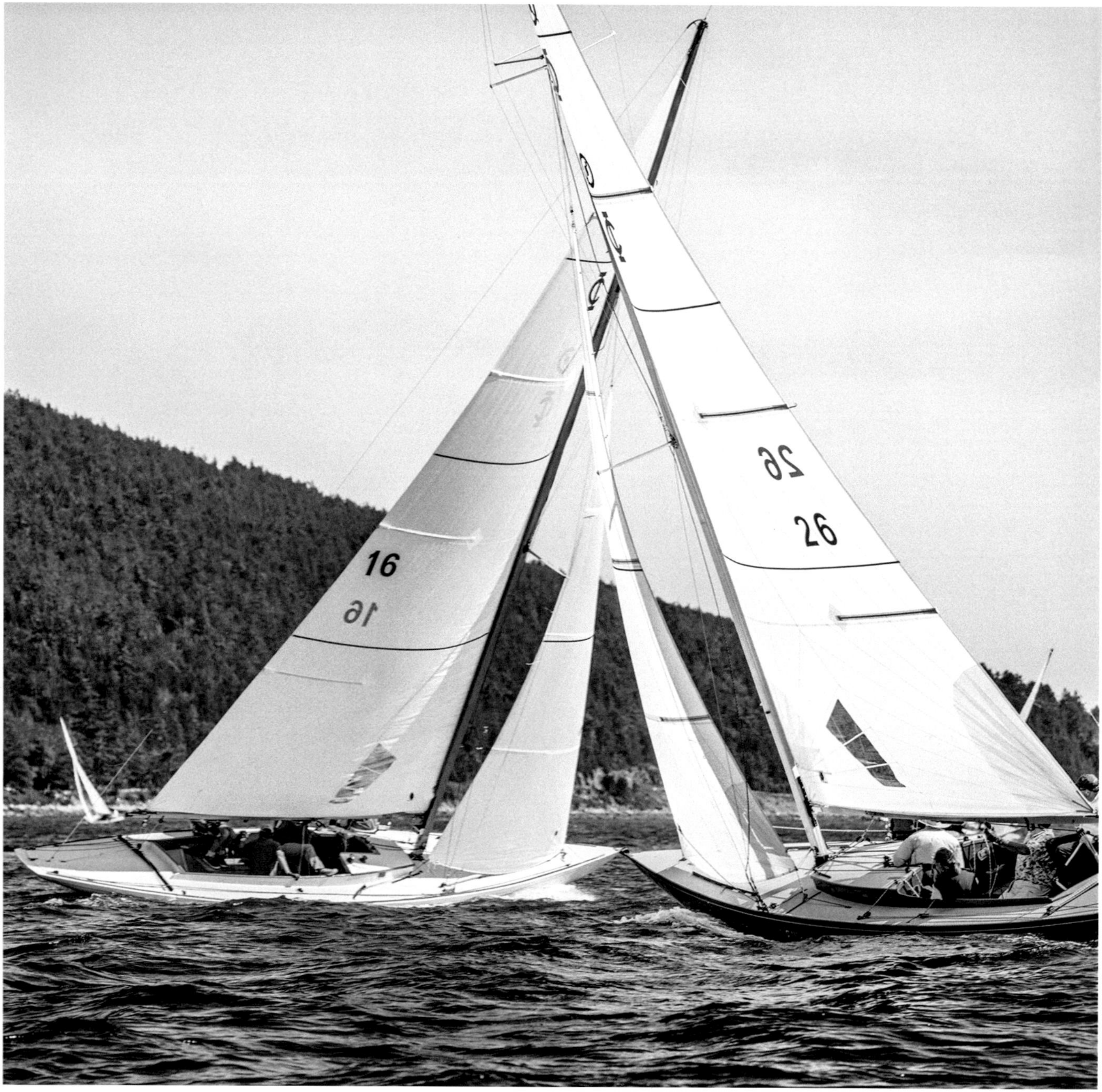

Somes Sound, 2003

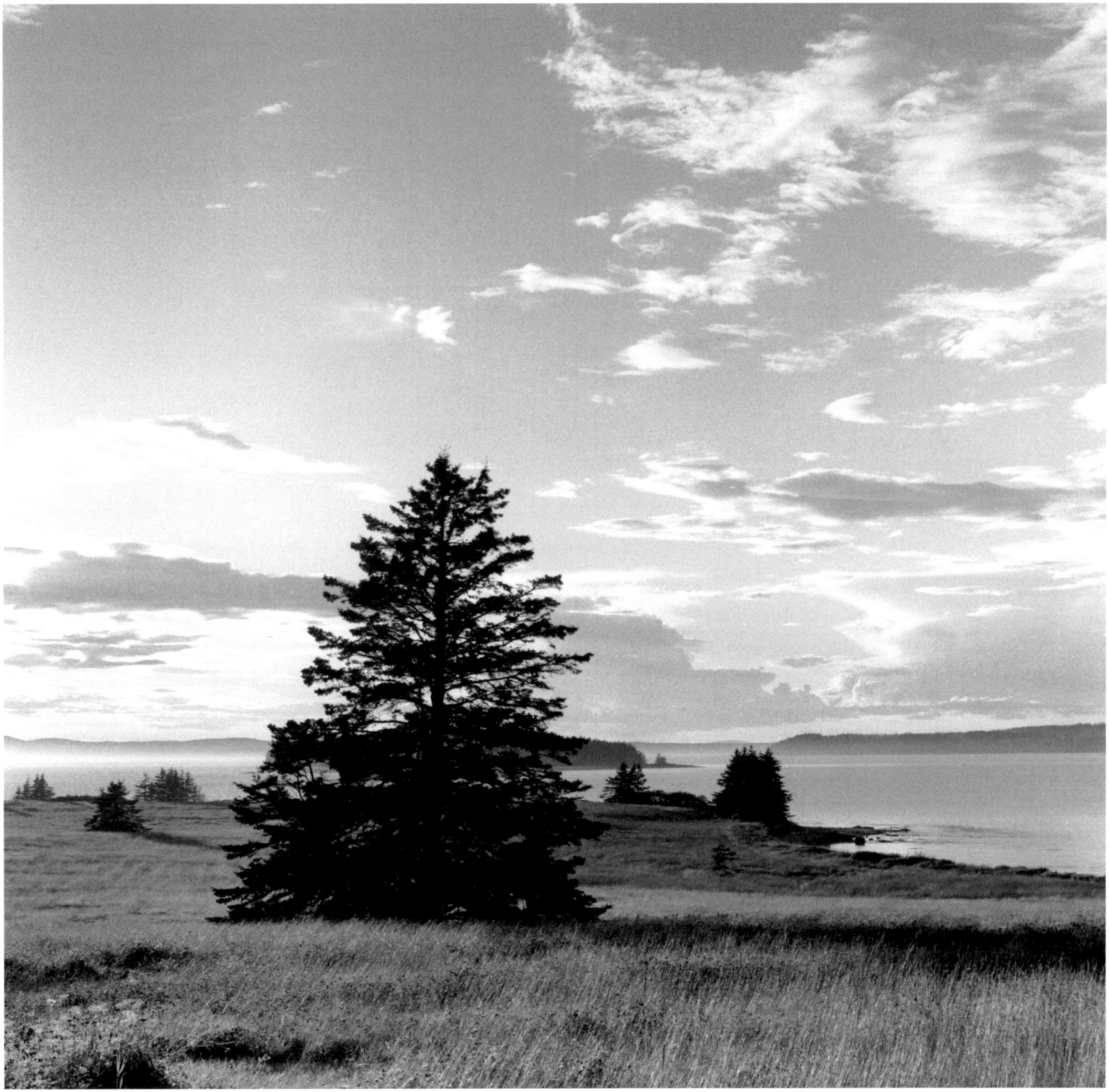

Hog Island, 2004

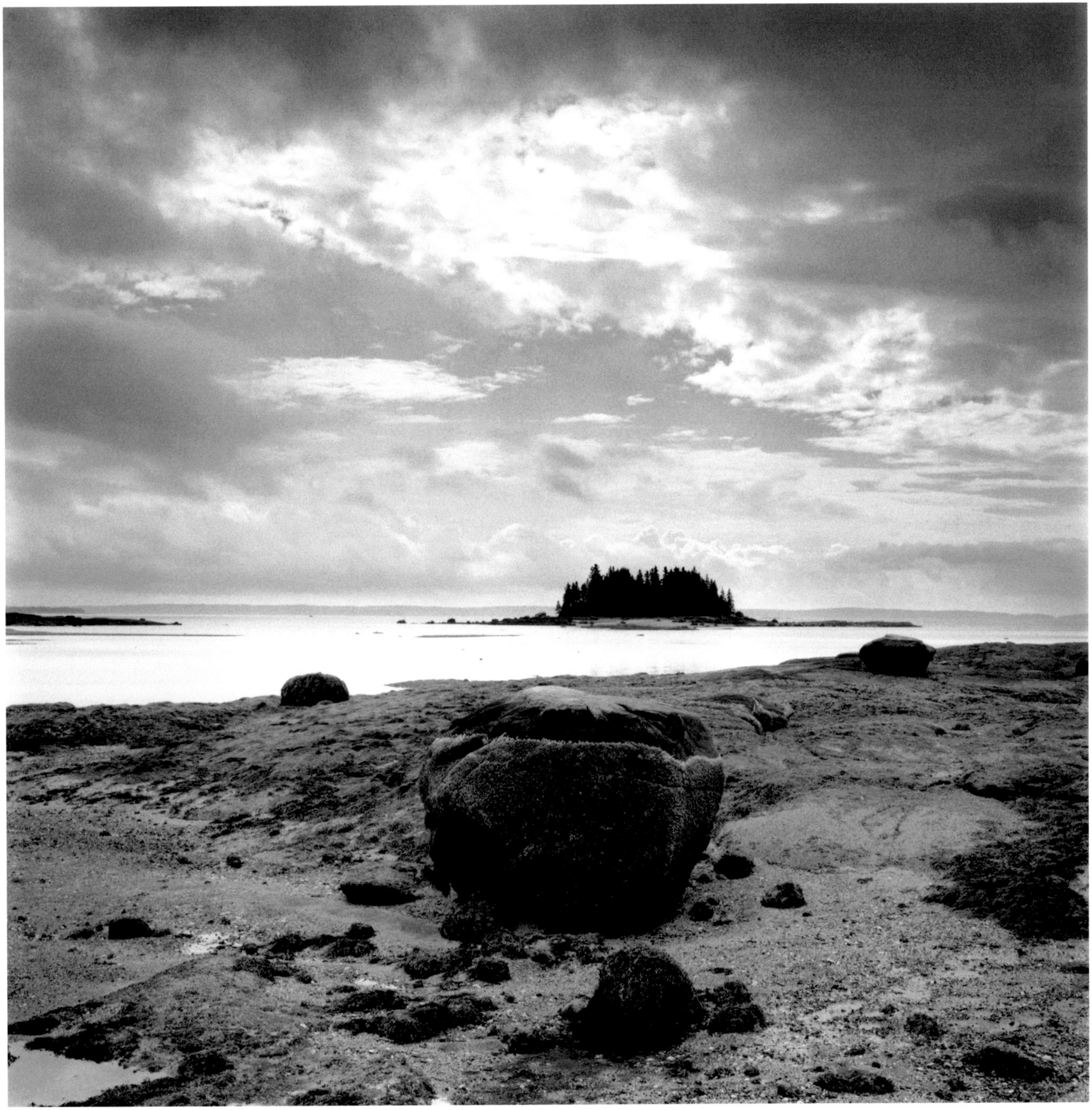

Blue Hill Bay, 2010

And all the loveliest things there be
Come simply, so, it seems to me.

—EDNA ST. VINCENT MILLAY

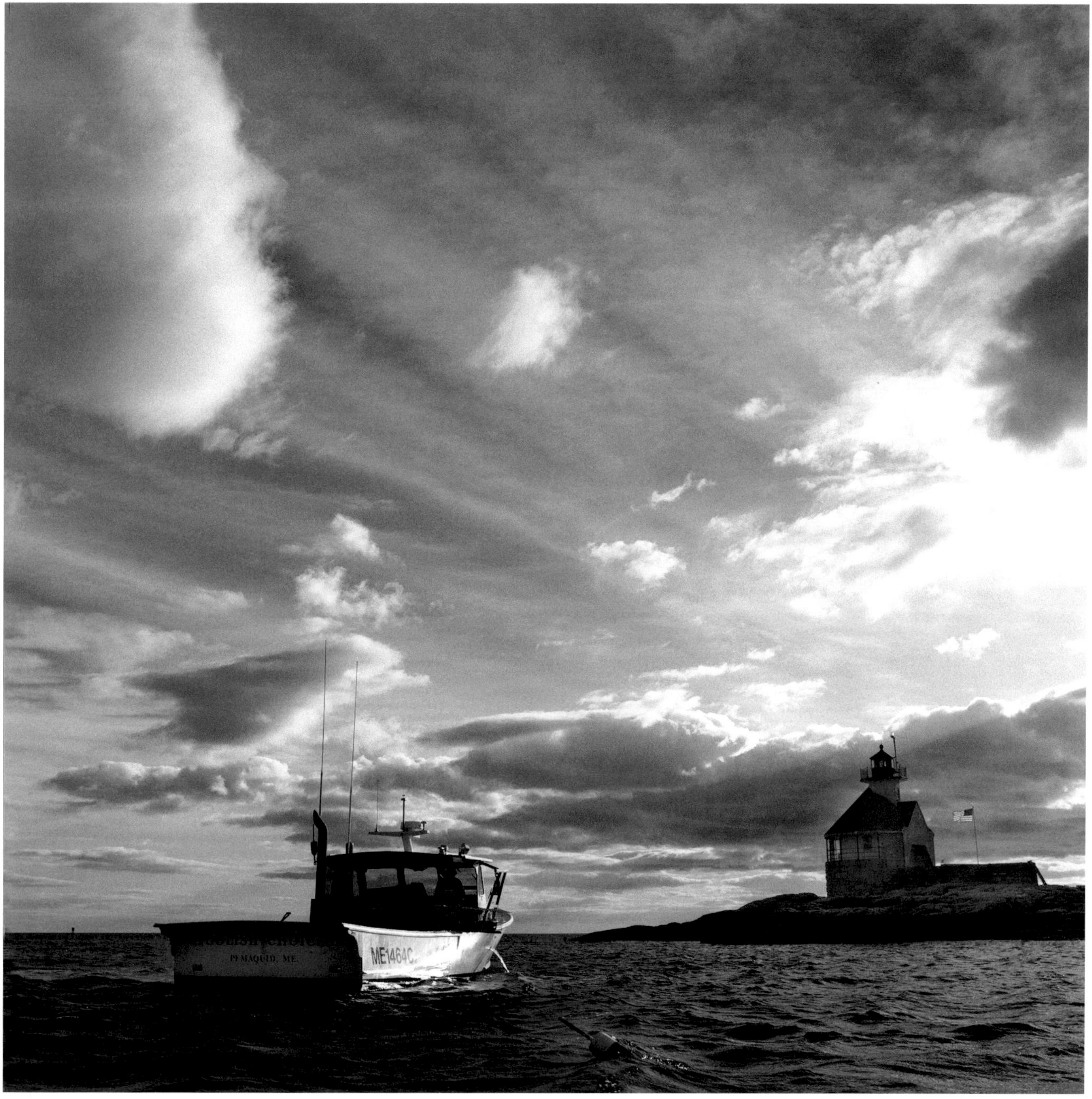

The Cuckolds, 2009

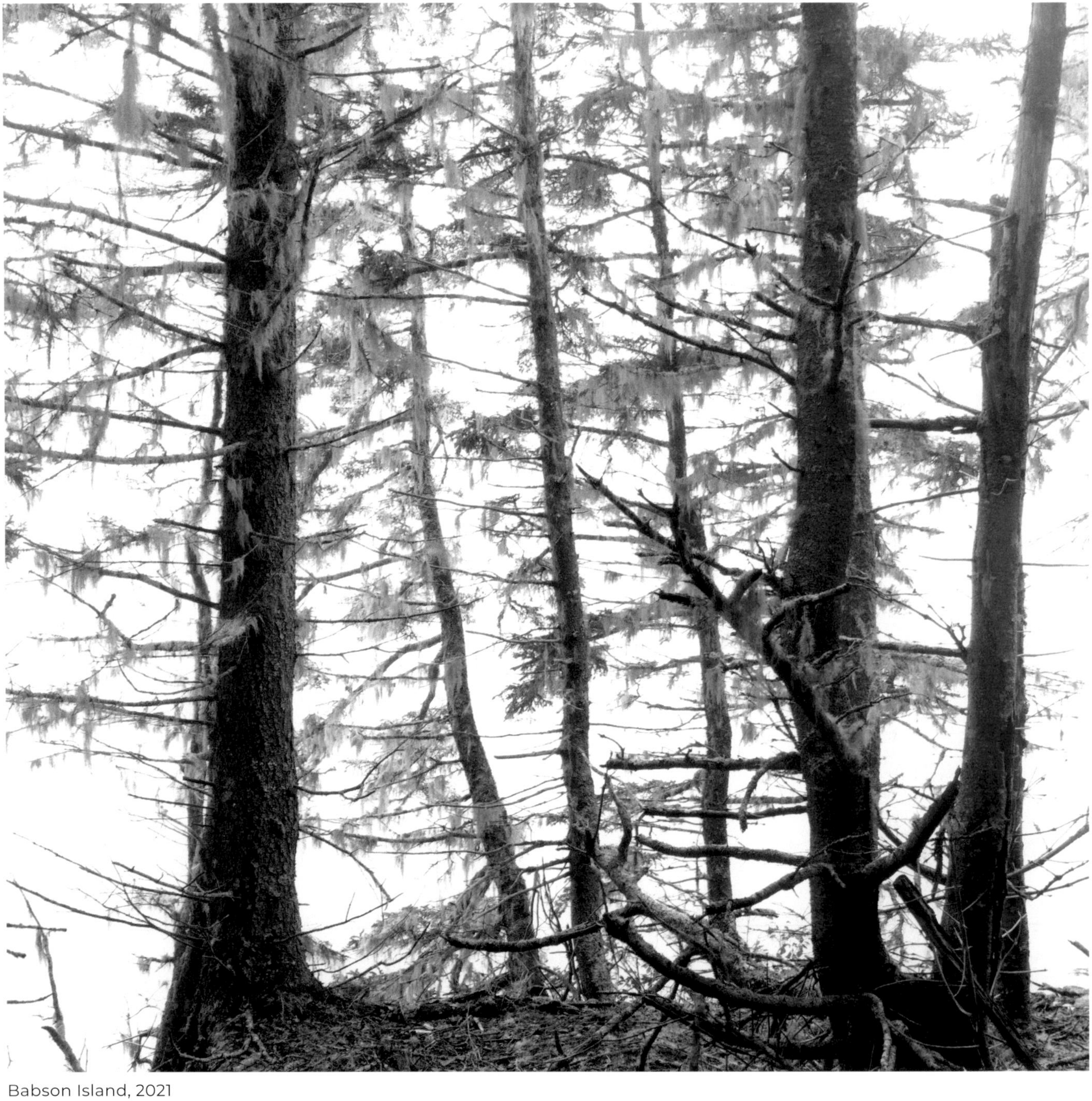

Babson Island, 2021

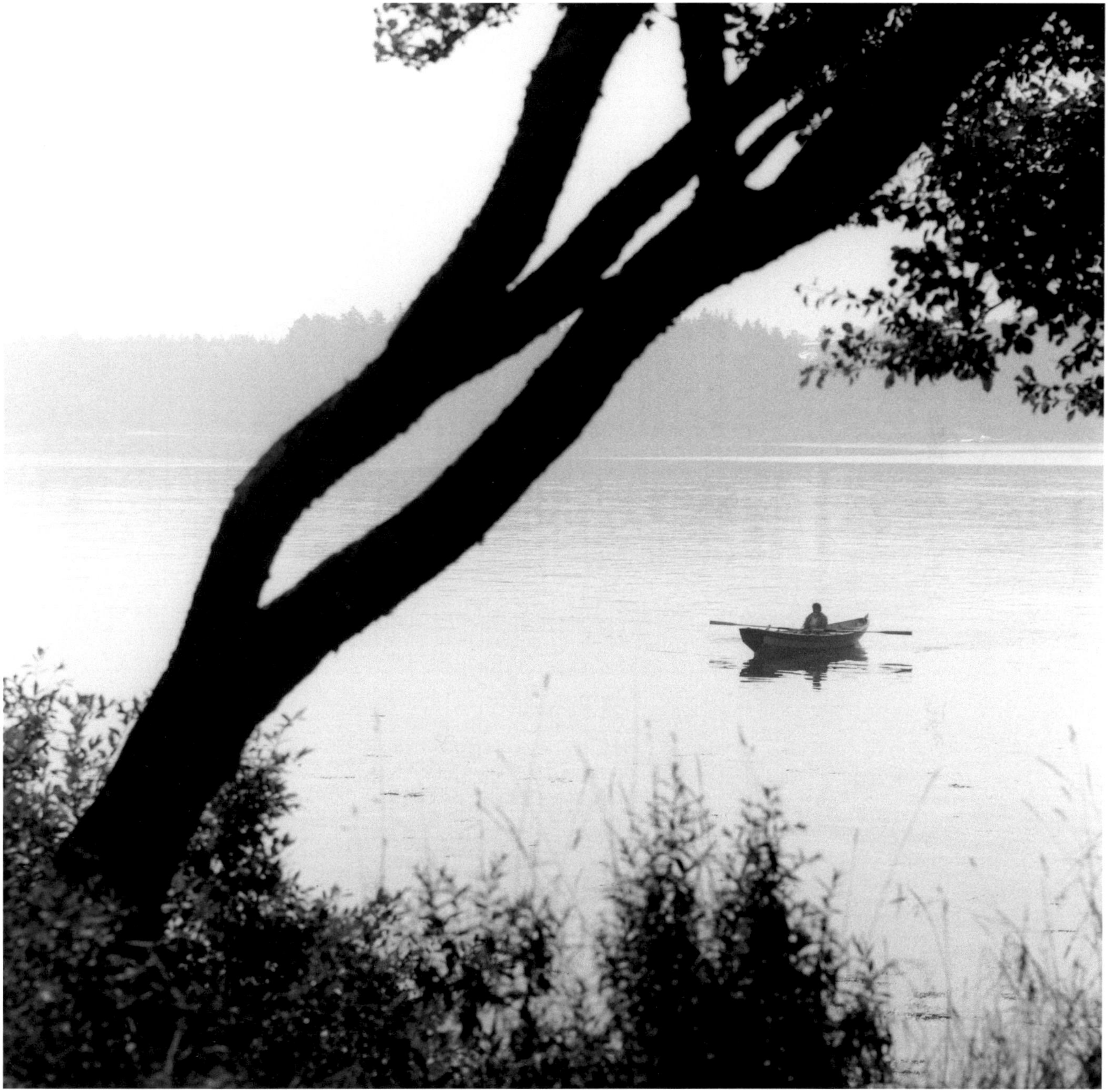

Brooklin, 2007

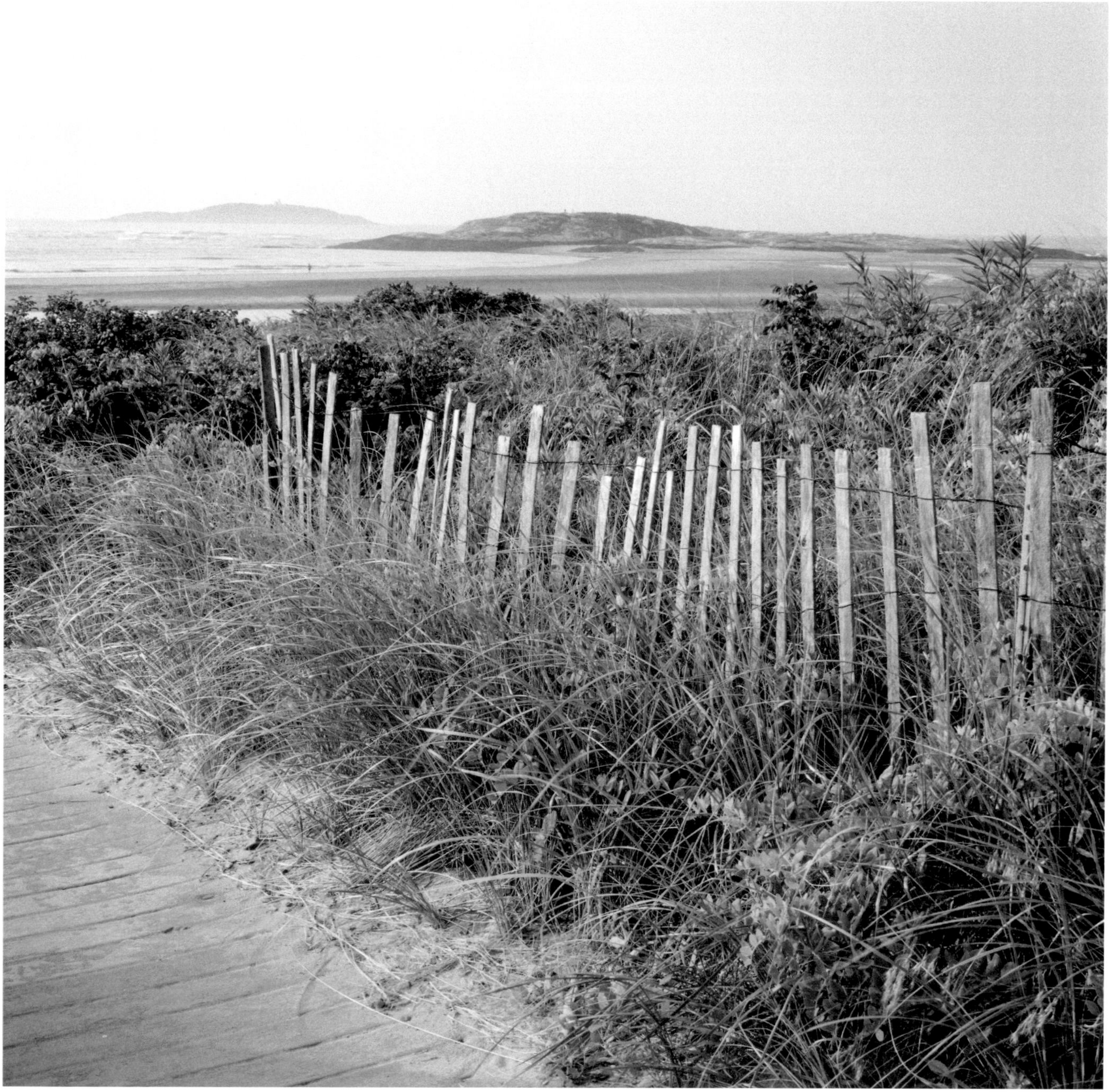

Popham Beach, 2006

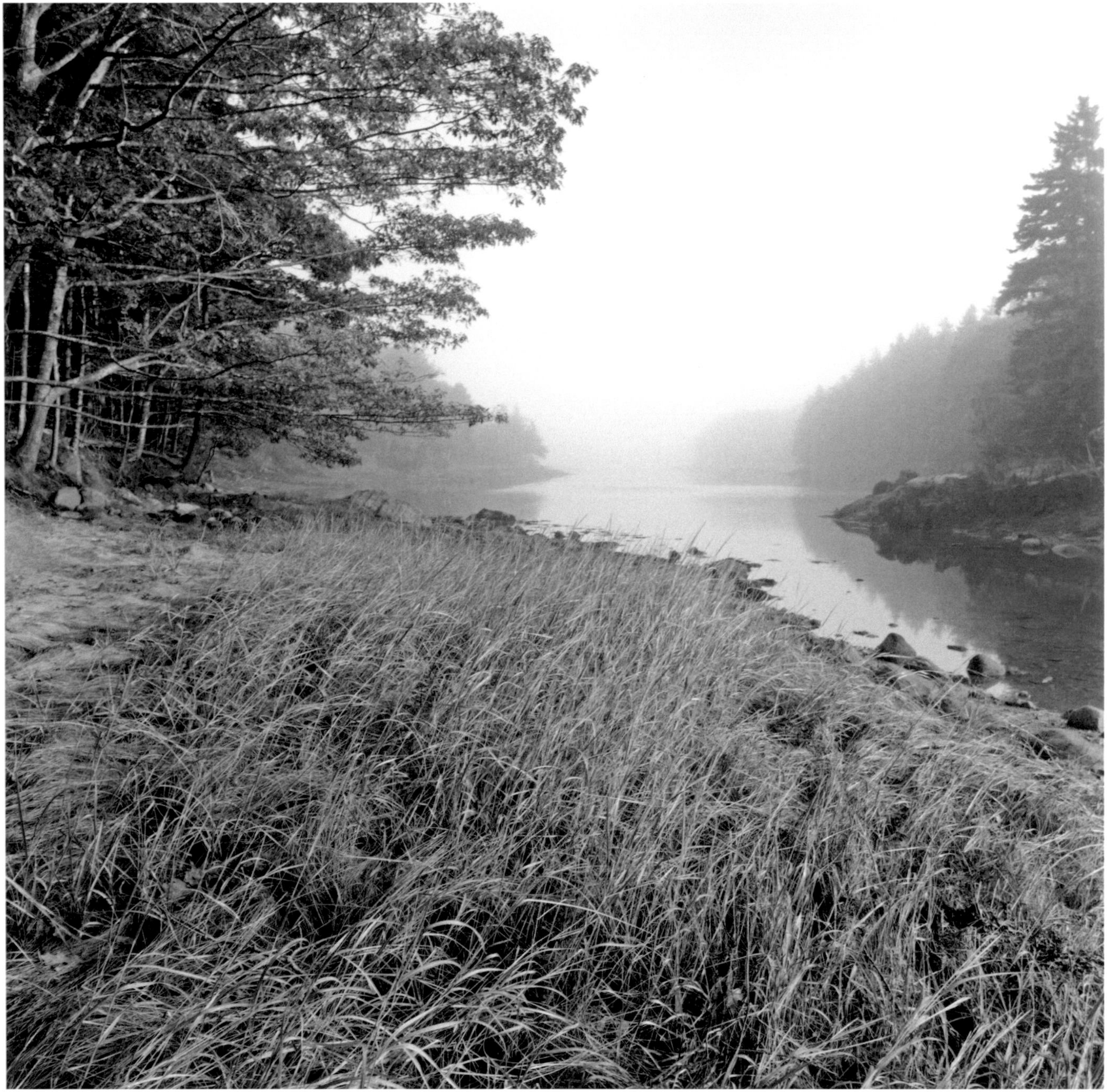

Little River, 2012

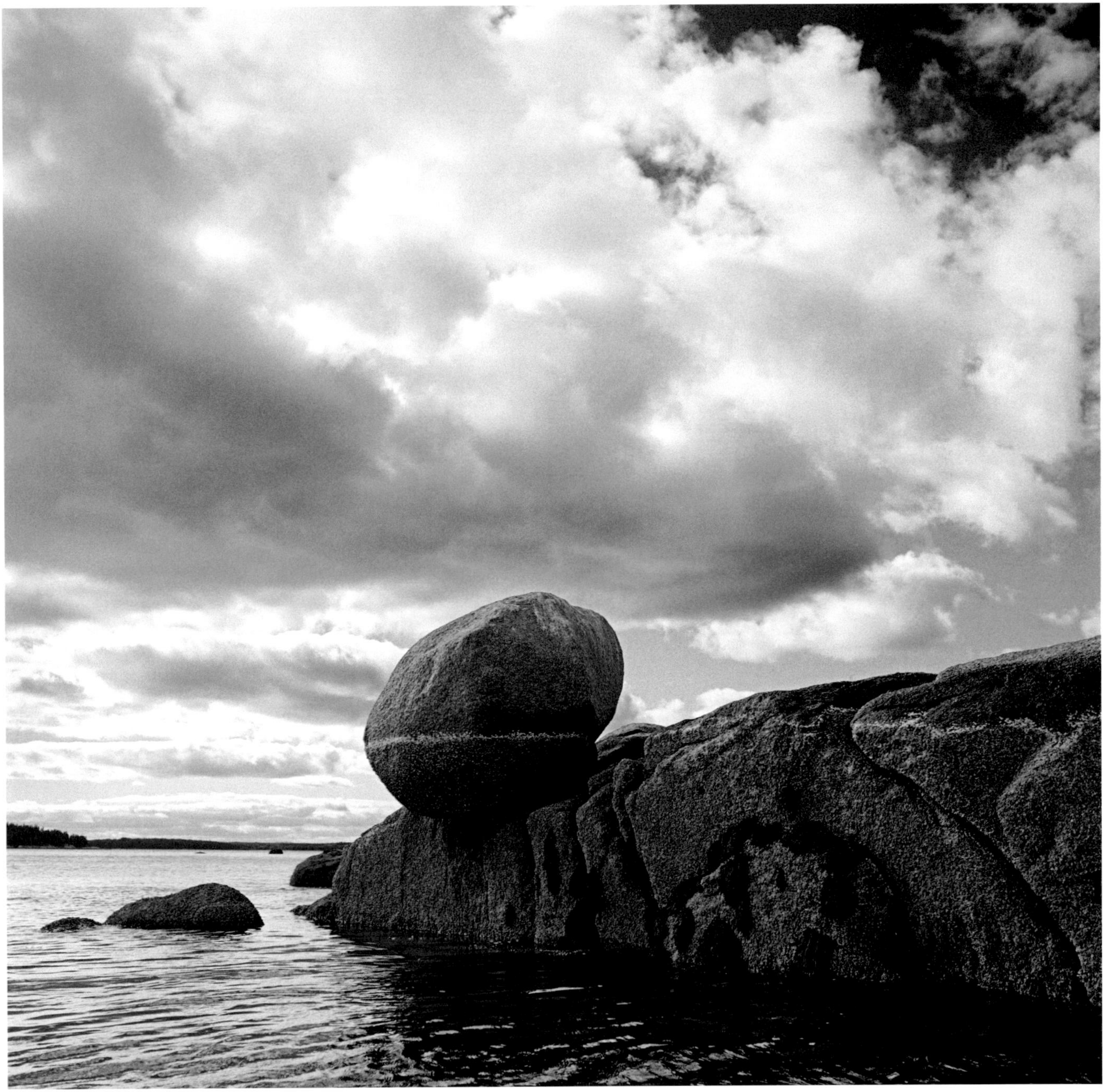

Babson Island, 2010

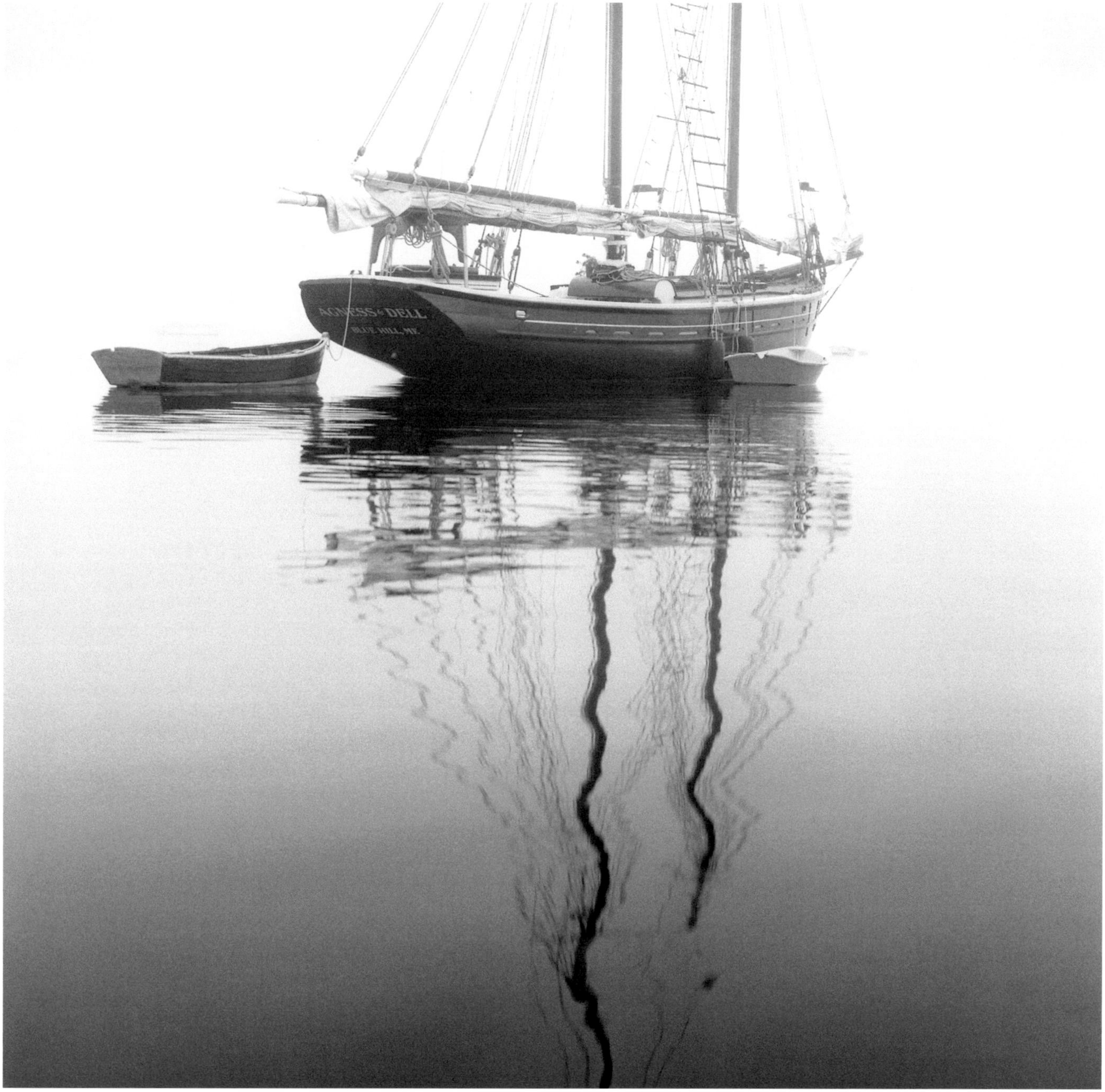

Blue Hill, 2003

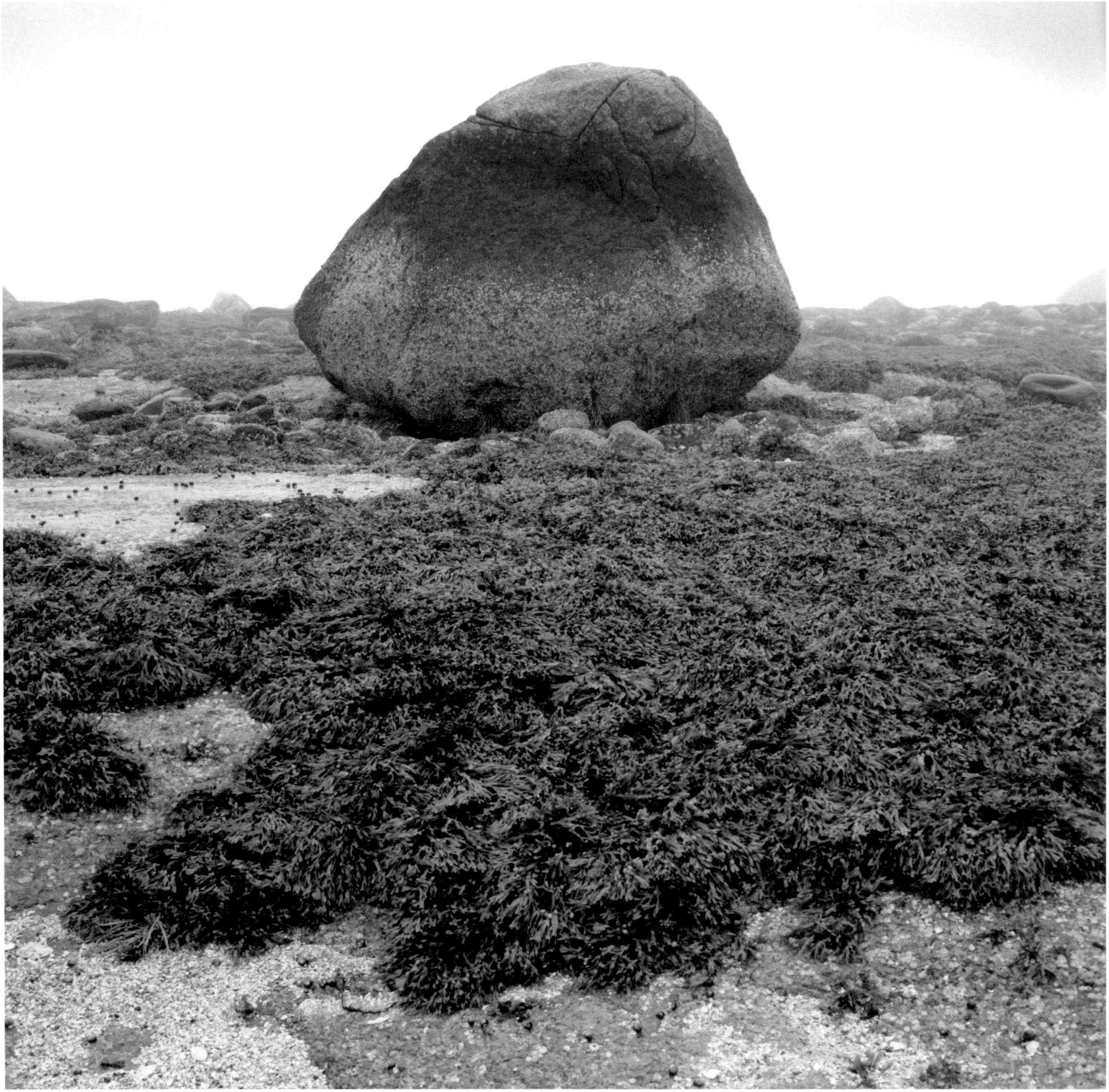

Hog Island, 2022

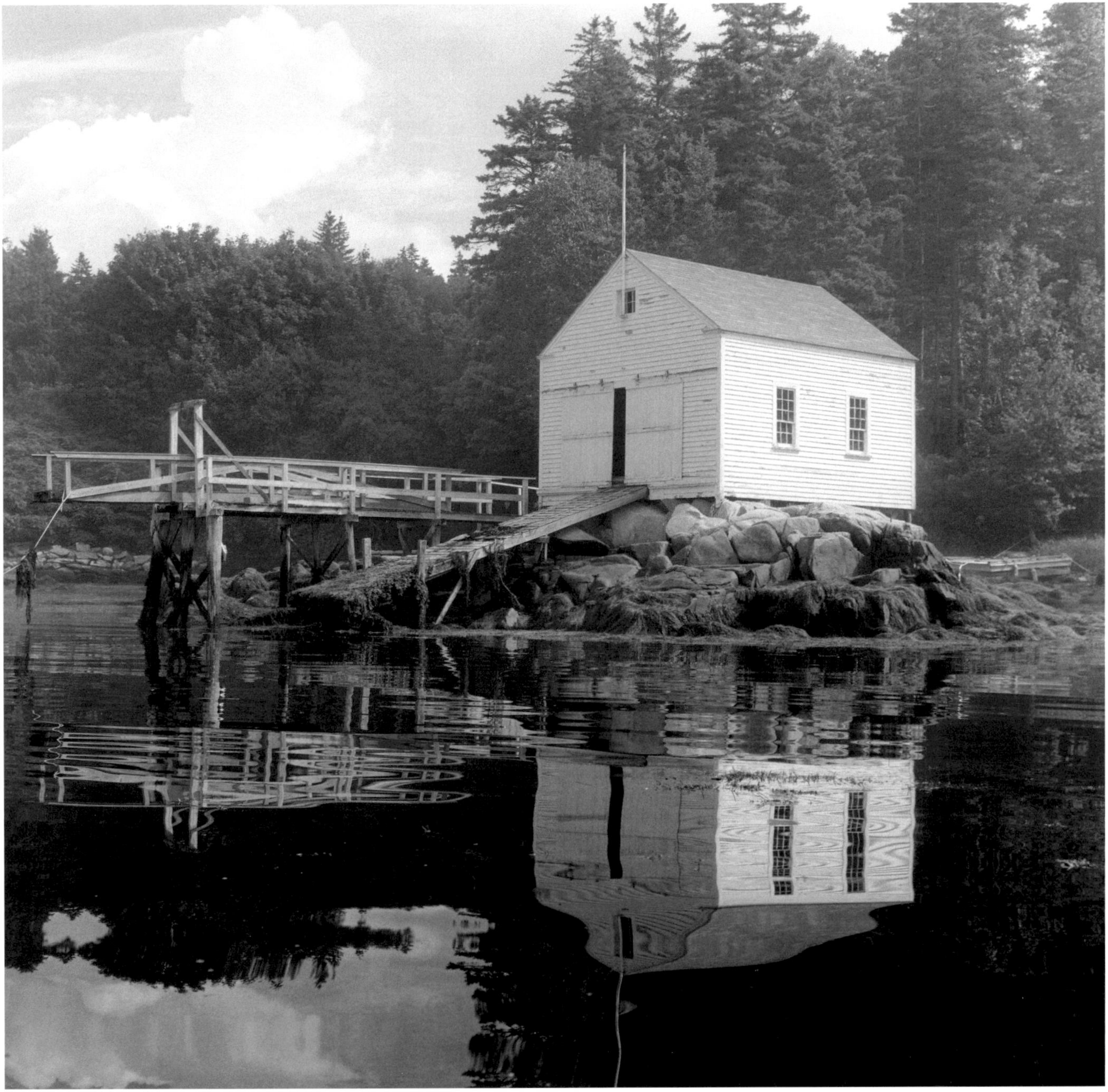

South Port, 2008

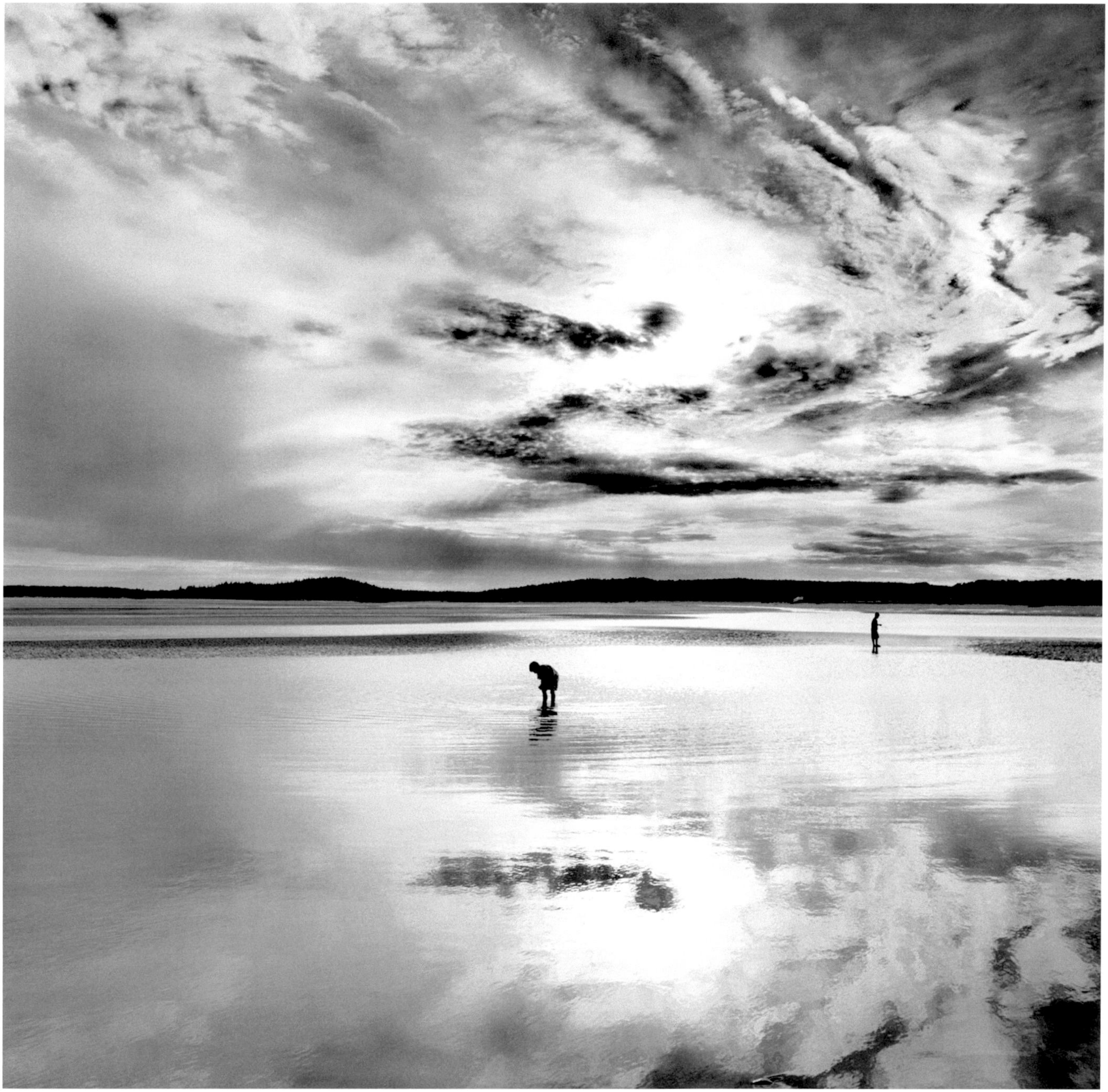

Popham Beach, 2002

You must live in the present, launch yourself on every wave, find your eternity in every moment.

—HENRY DAVID THOREAU

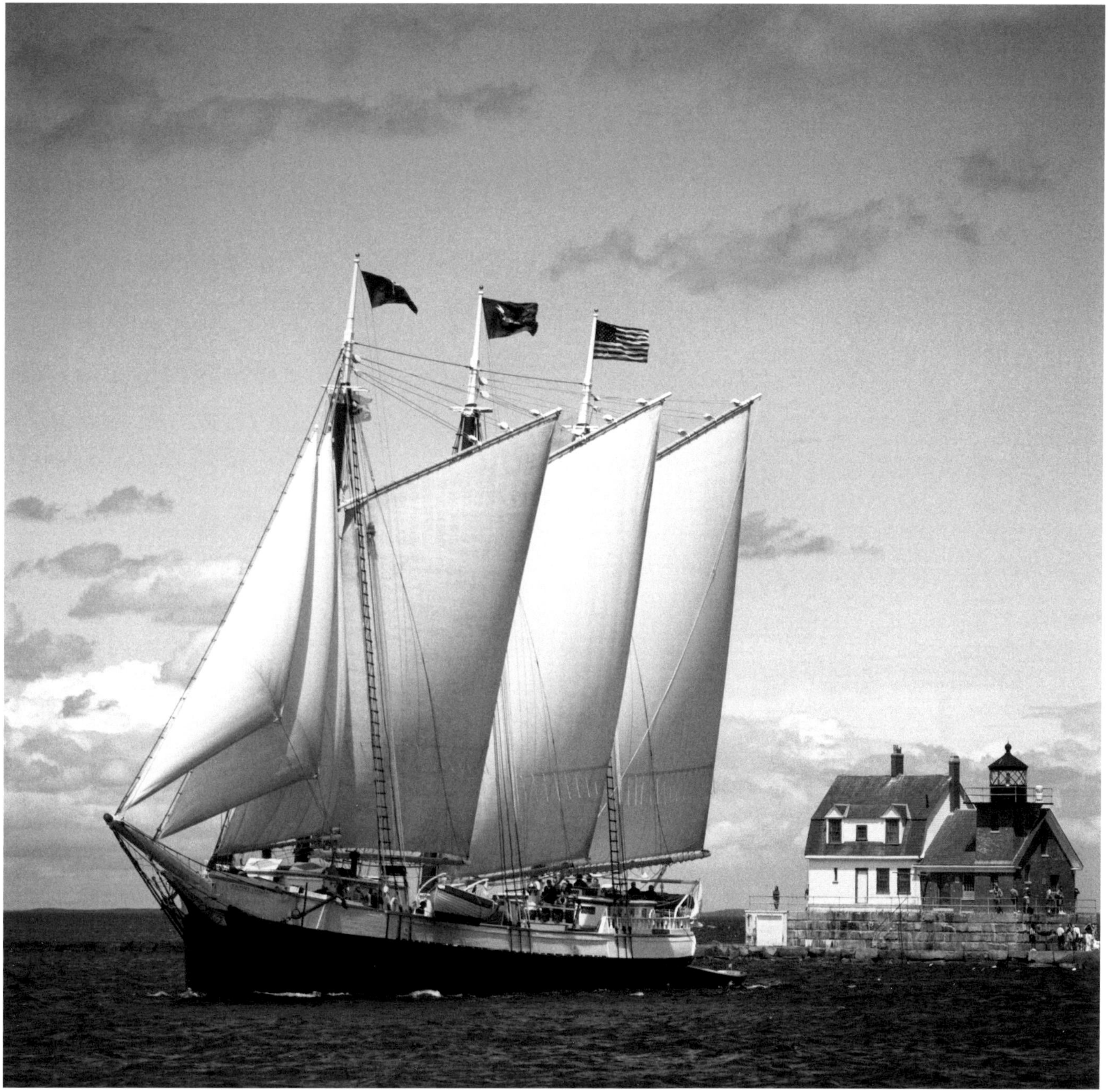

Rockland Breakwater Light, 1998

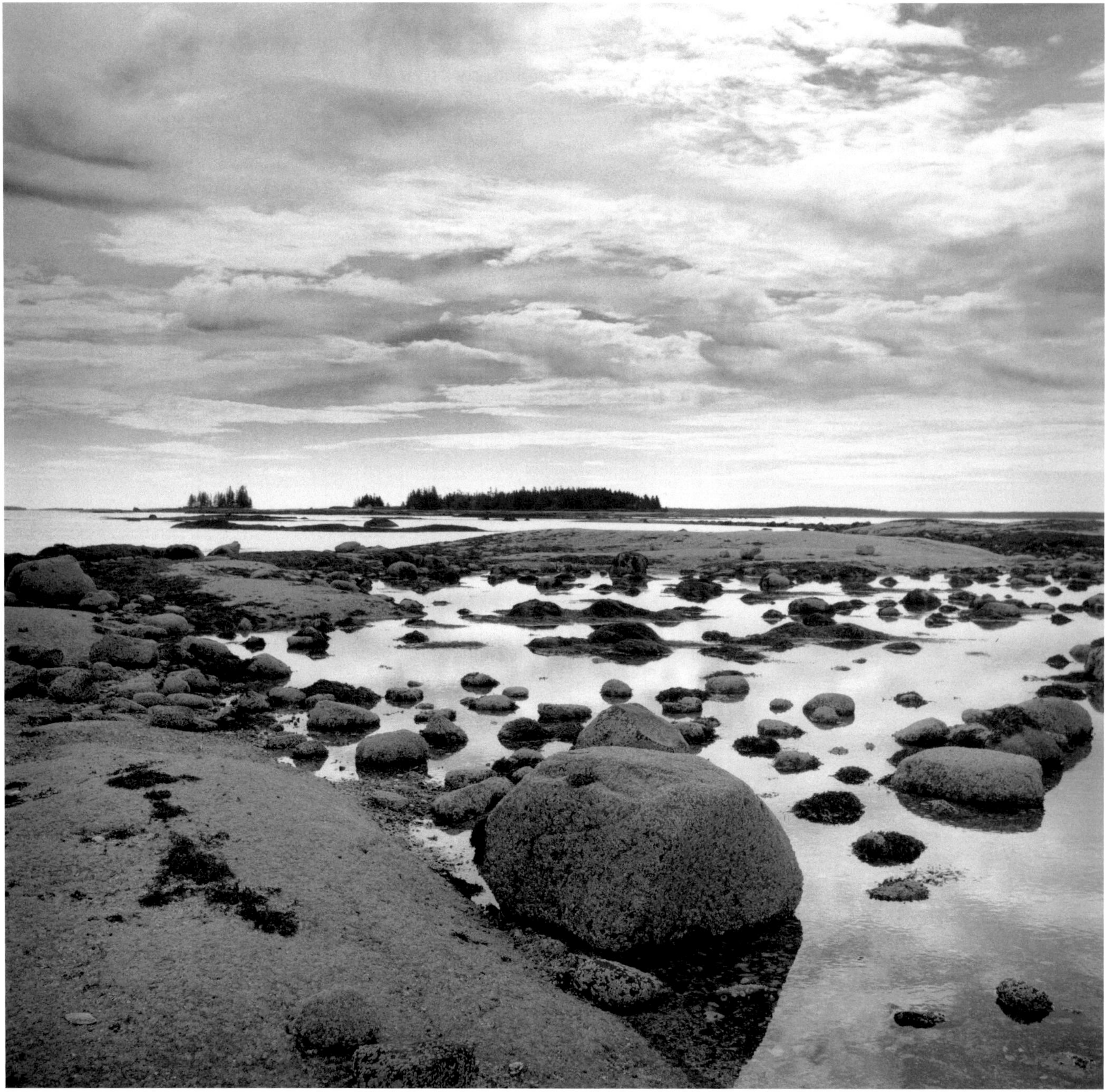

Flye Point, 2021

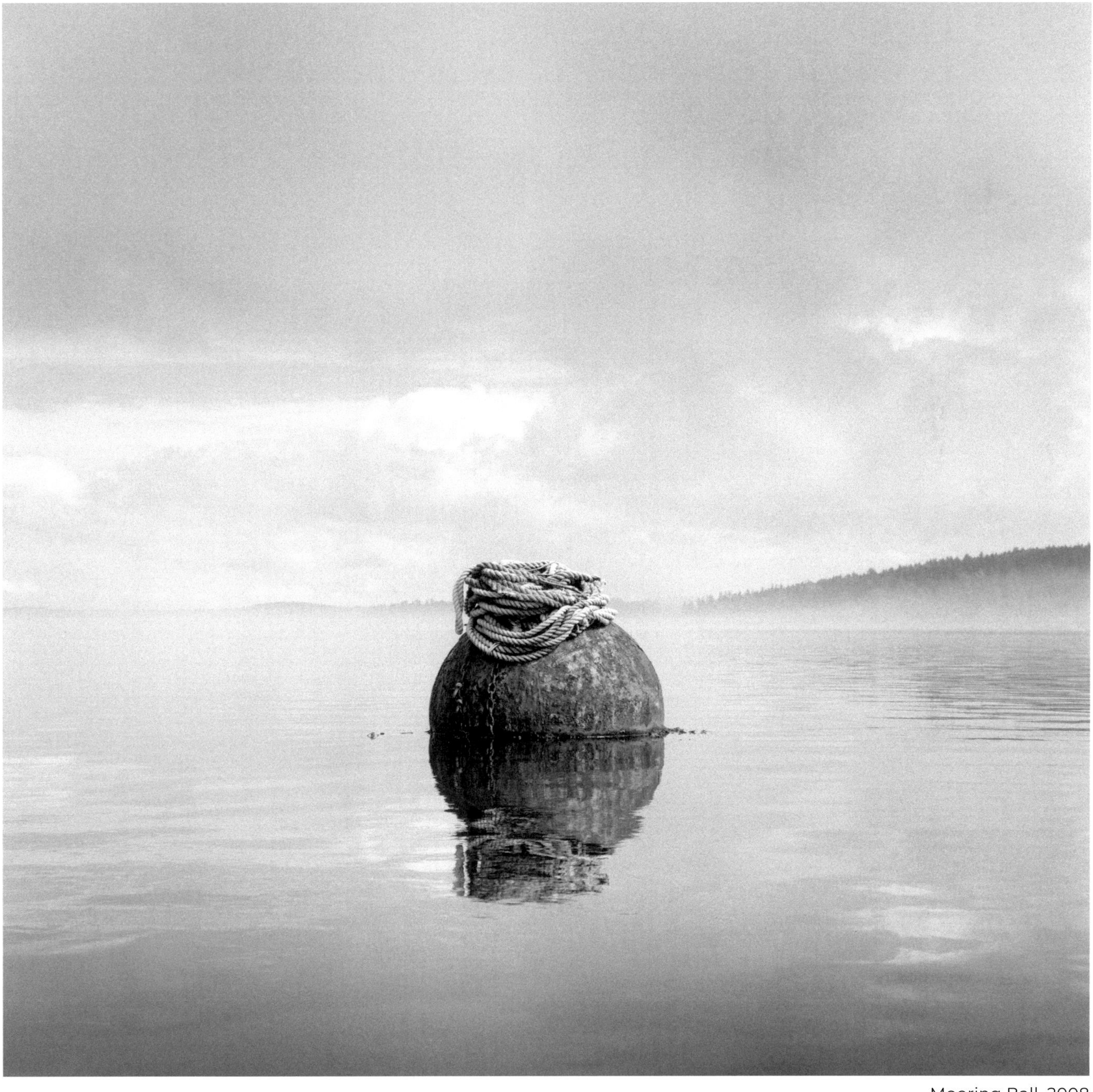

Mooring Ball, 2008

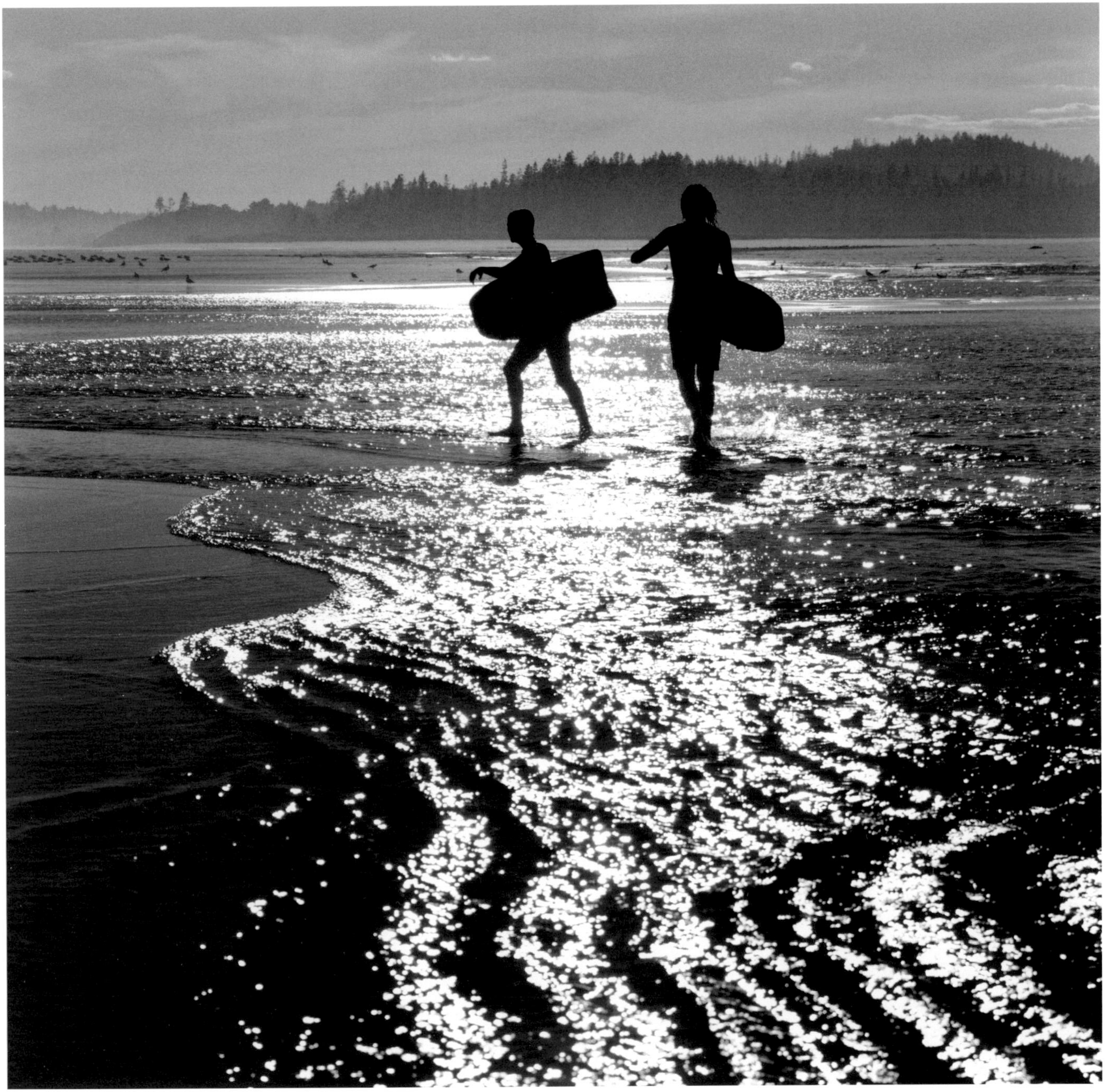

Popham Beach, 2011

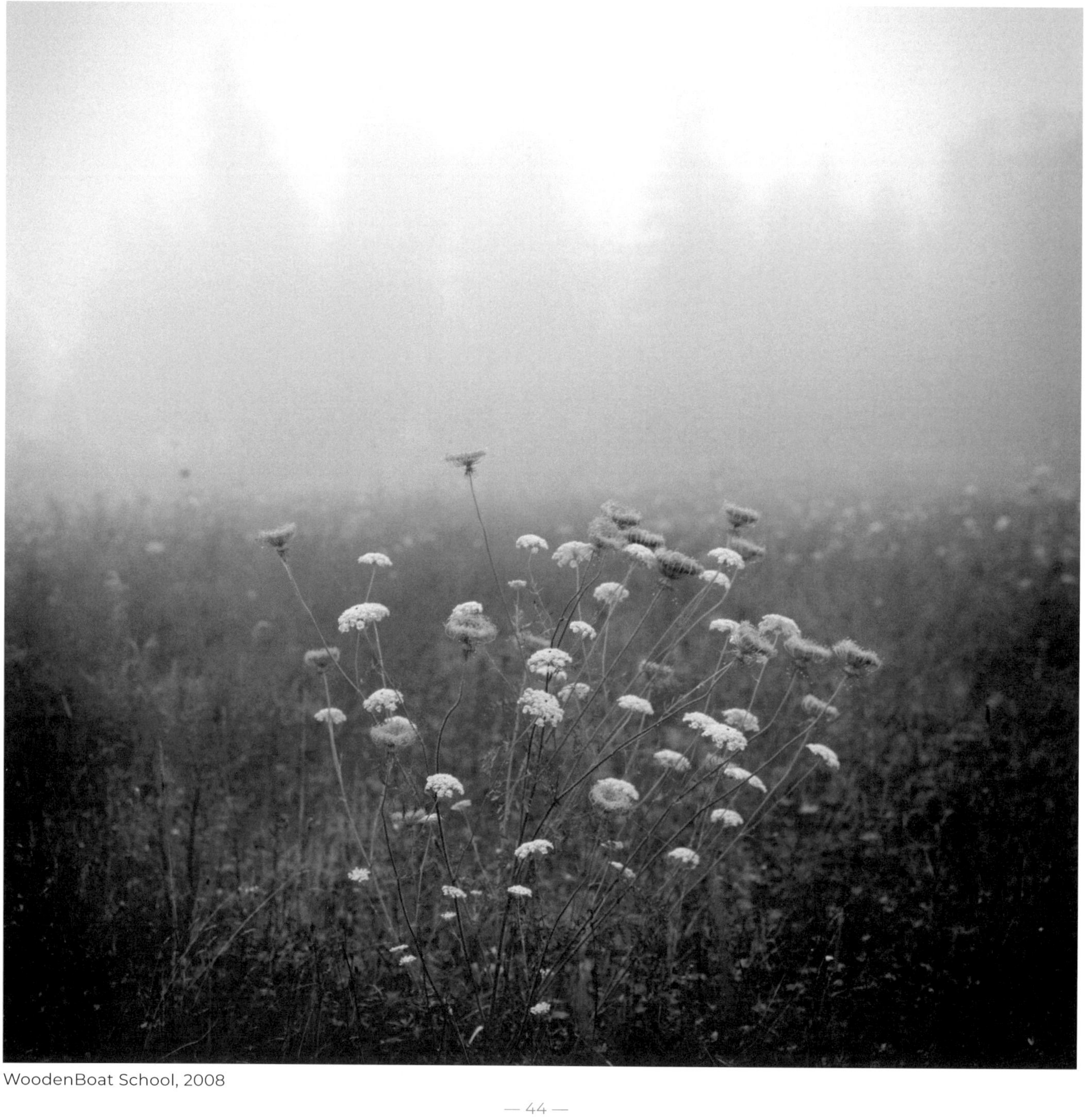

WoodenBoat School, 2008

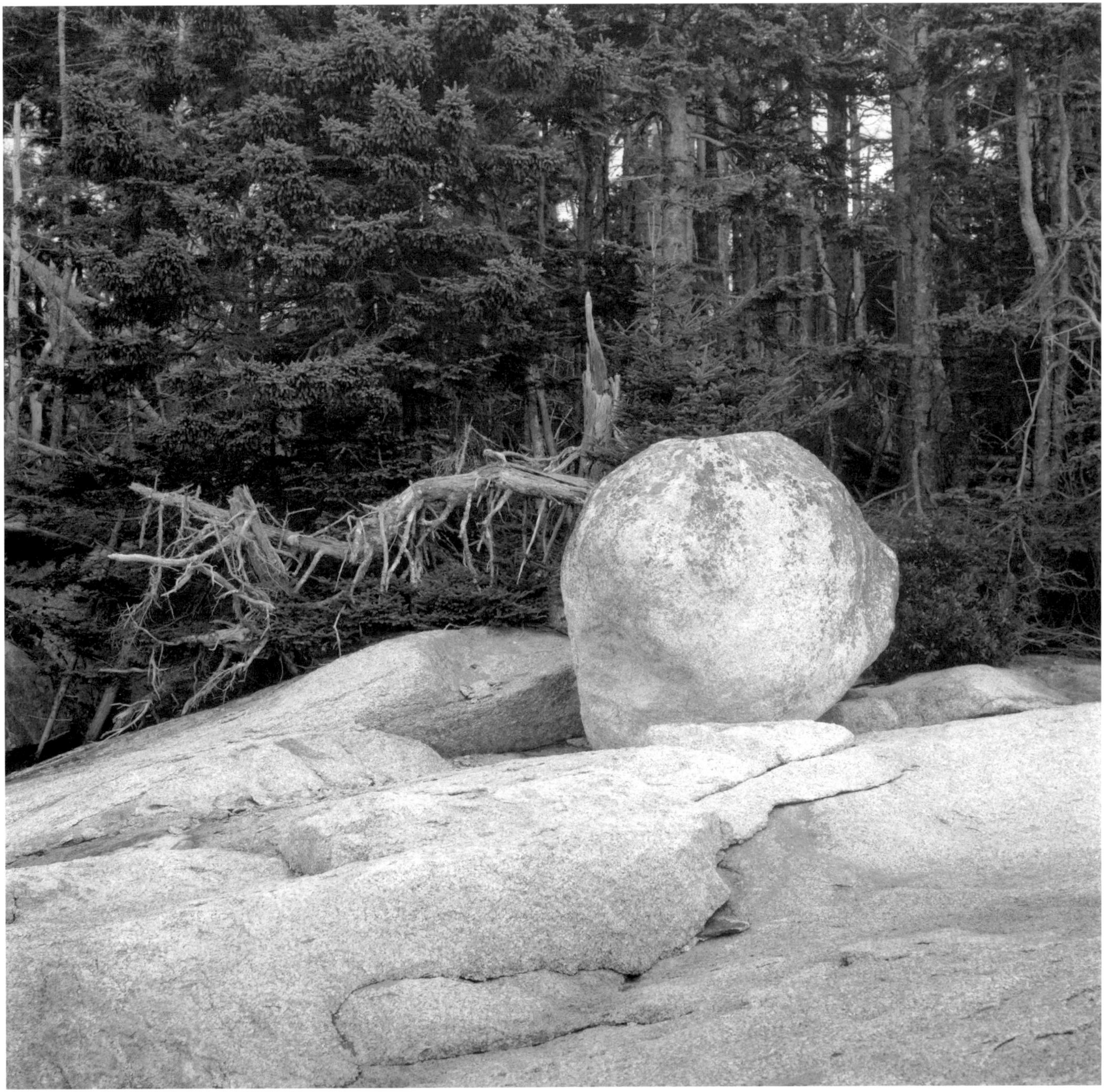

Harbor Island, 2022

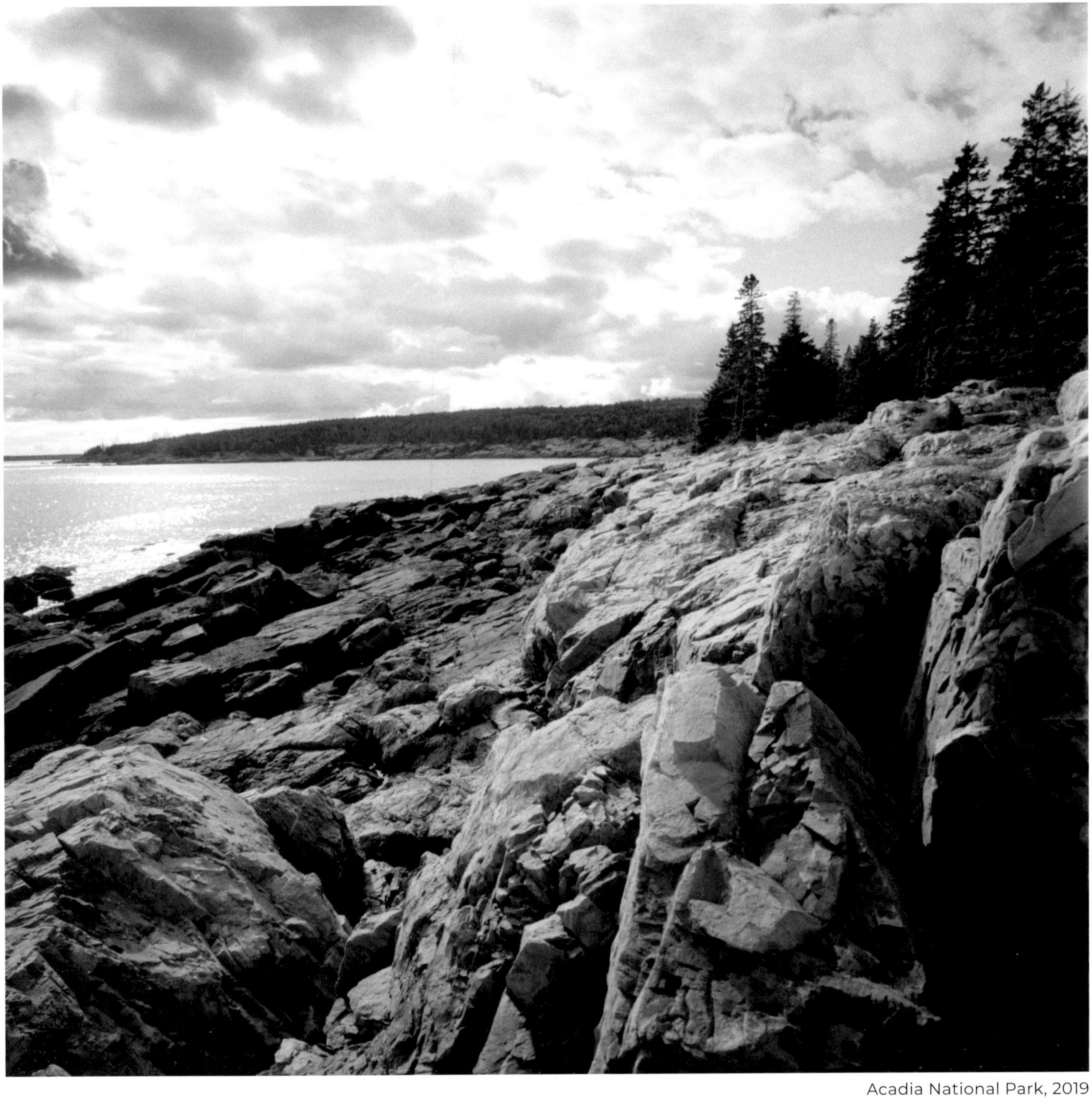

Acadia National Park, 2019

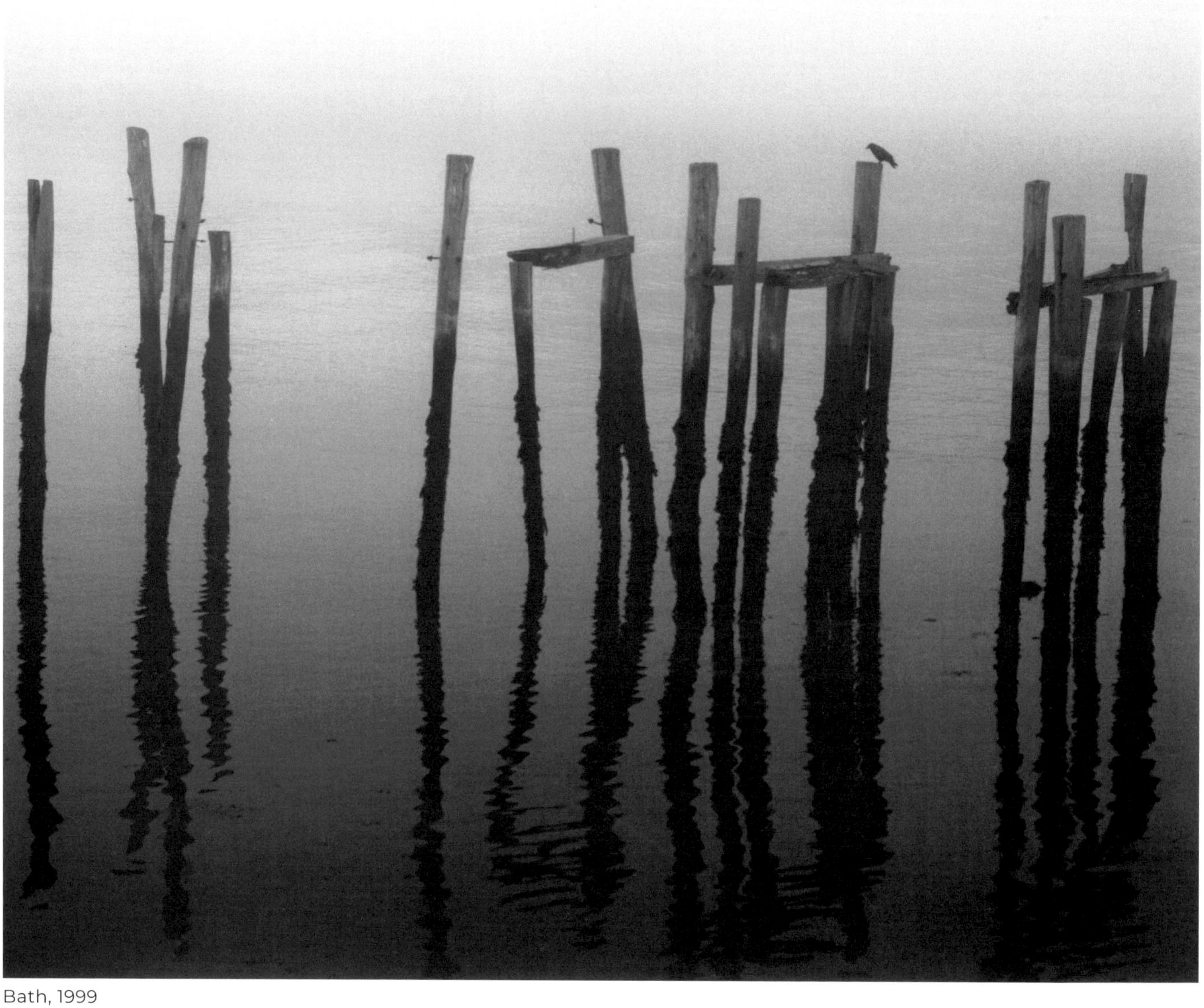

Bath, 1999

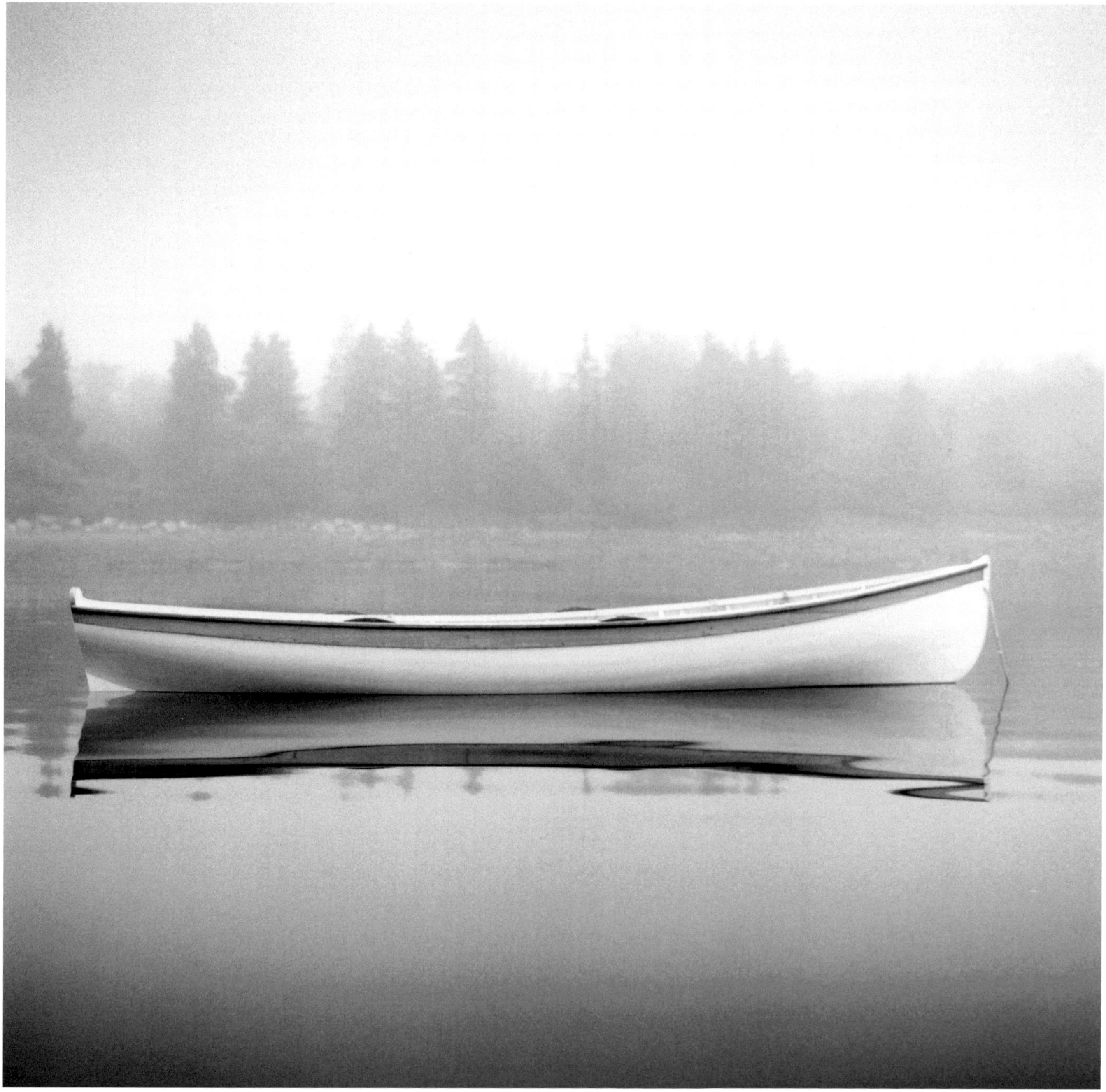

Brooklin, 2002

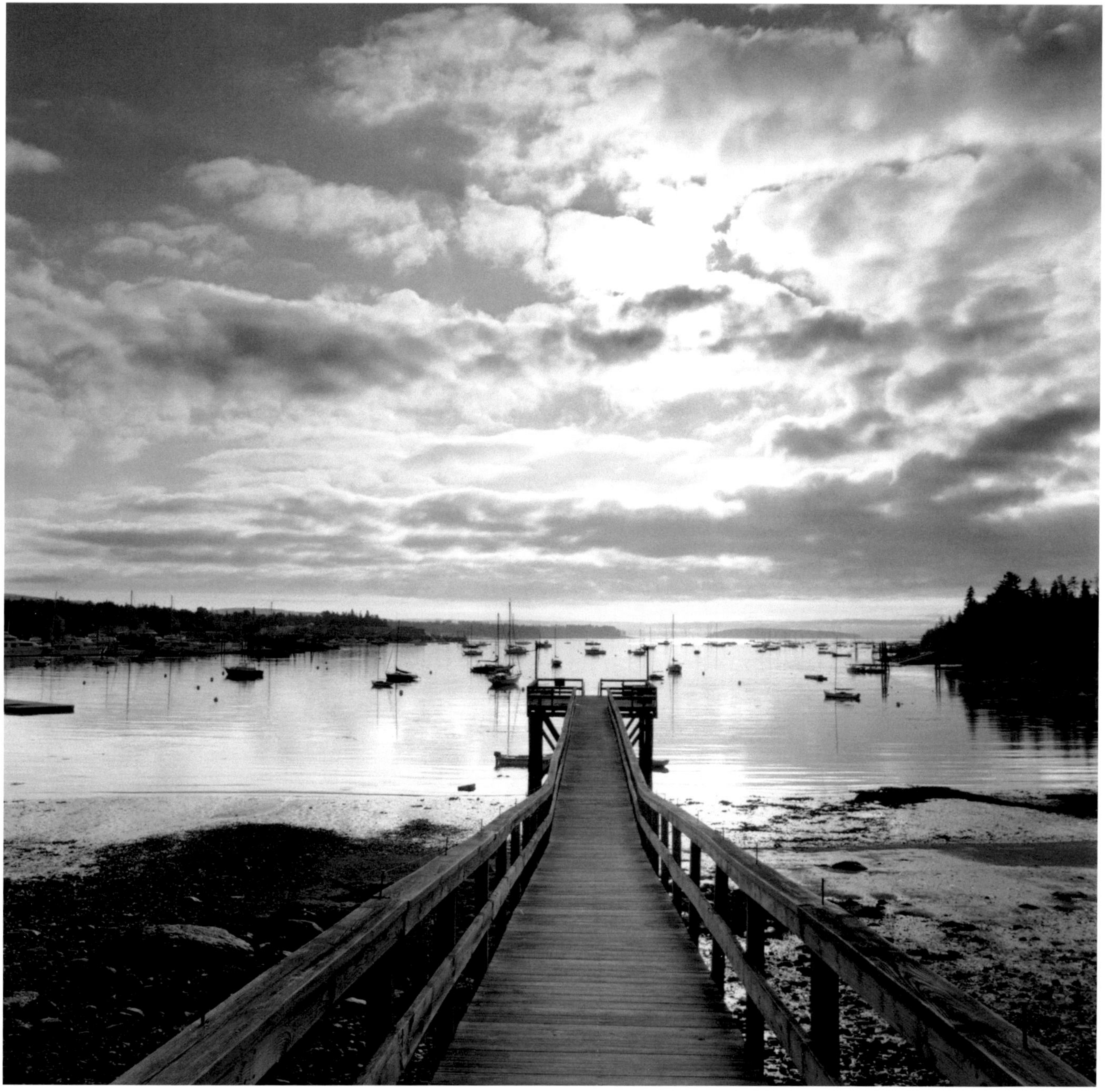

Southeast Harbor, 2011

Always be on the lookout for the presence of wonder.

—E. B. WHITE

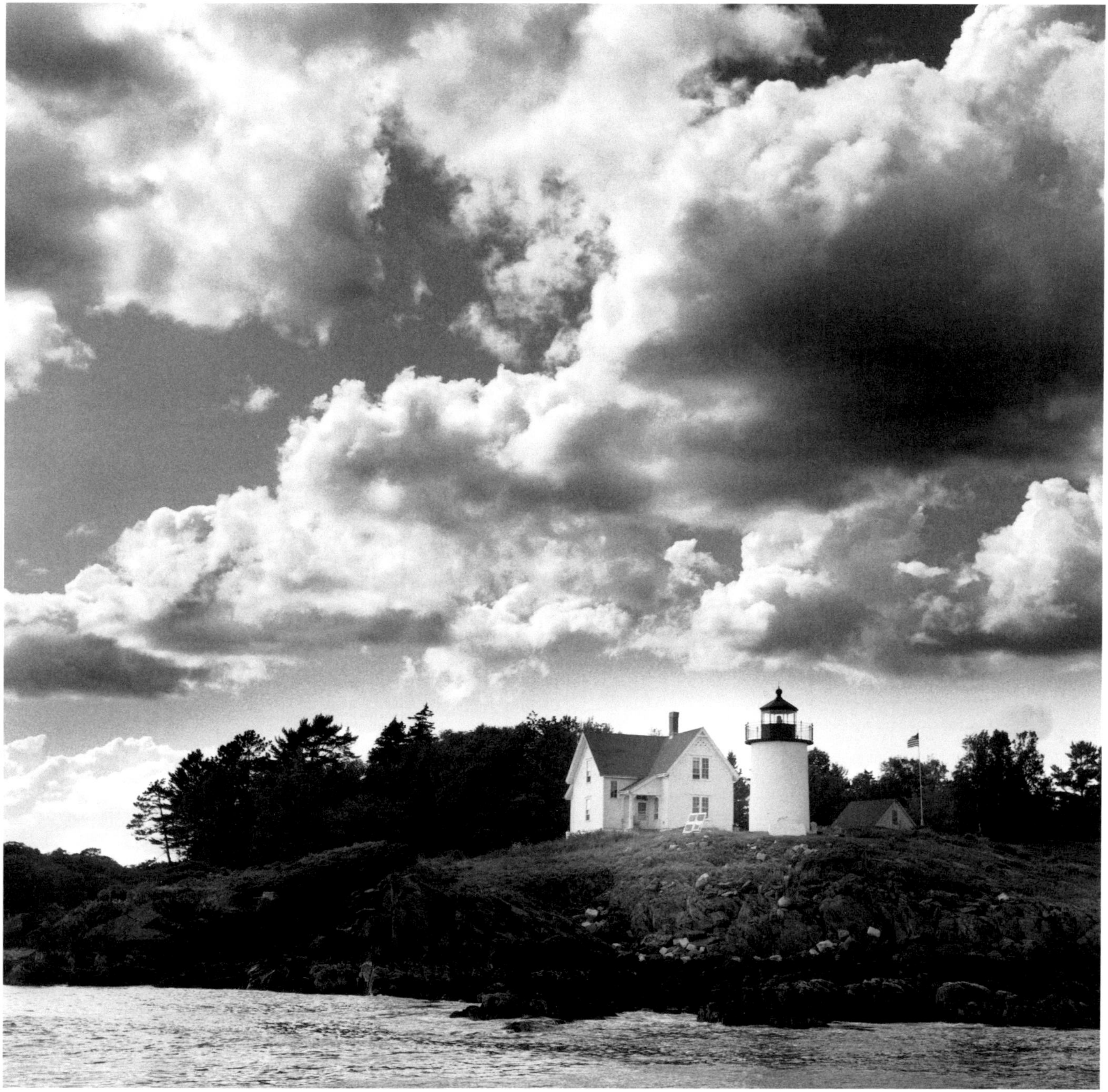

Curtis Island Light, 1998

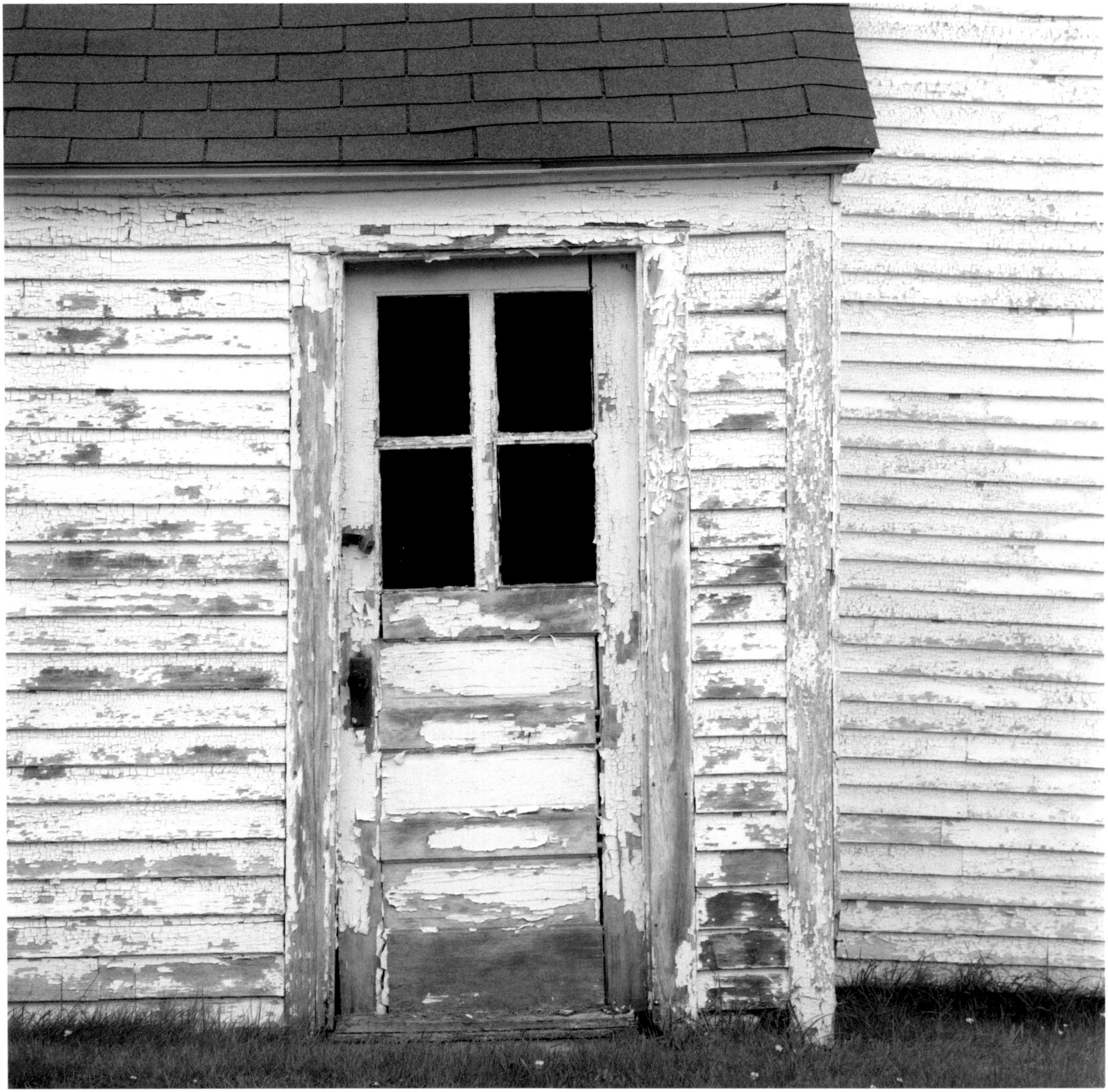

Brooklin, 2021

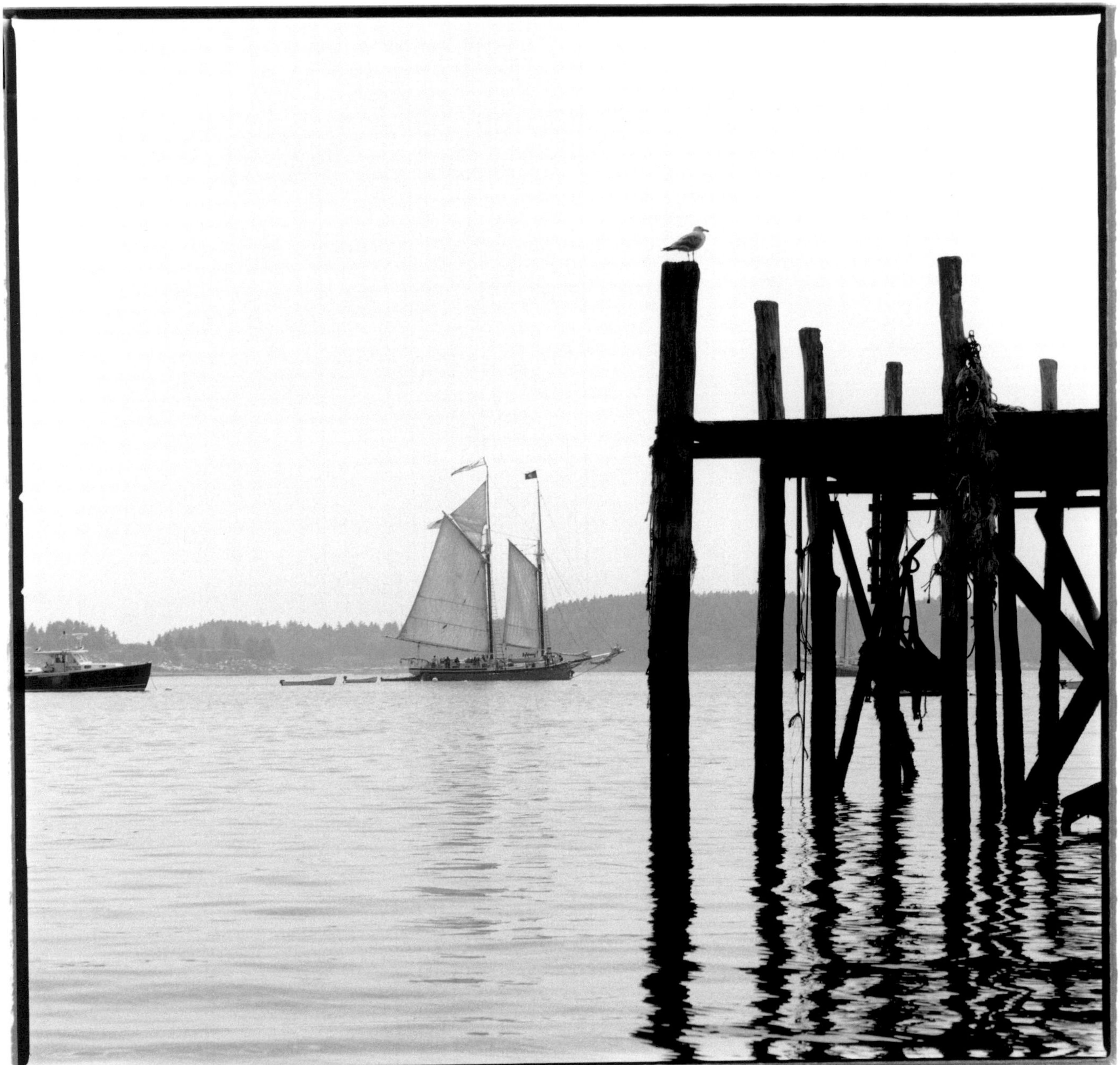

Stonington, 2010

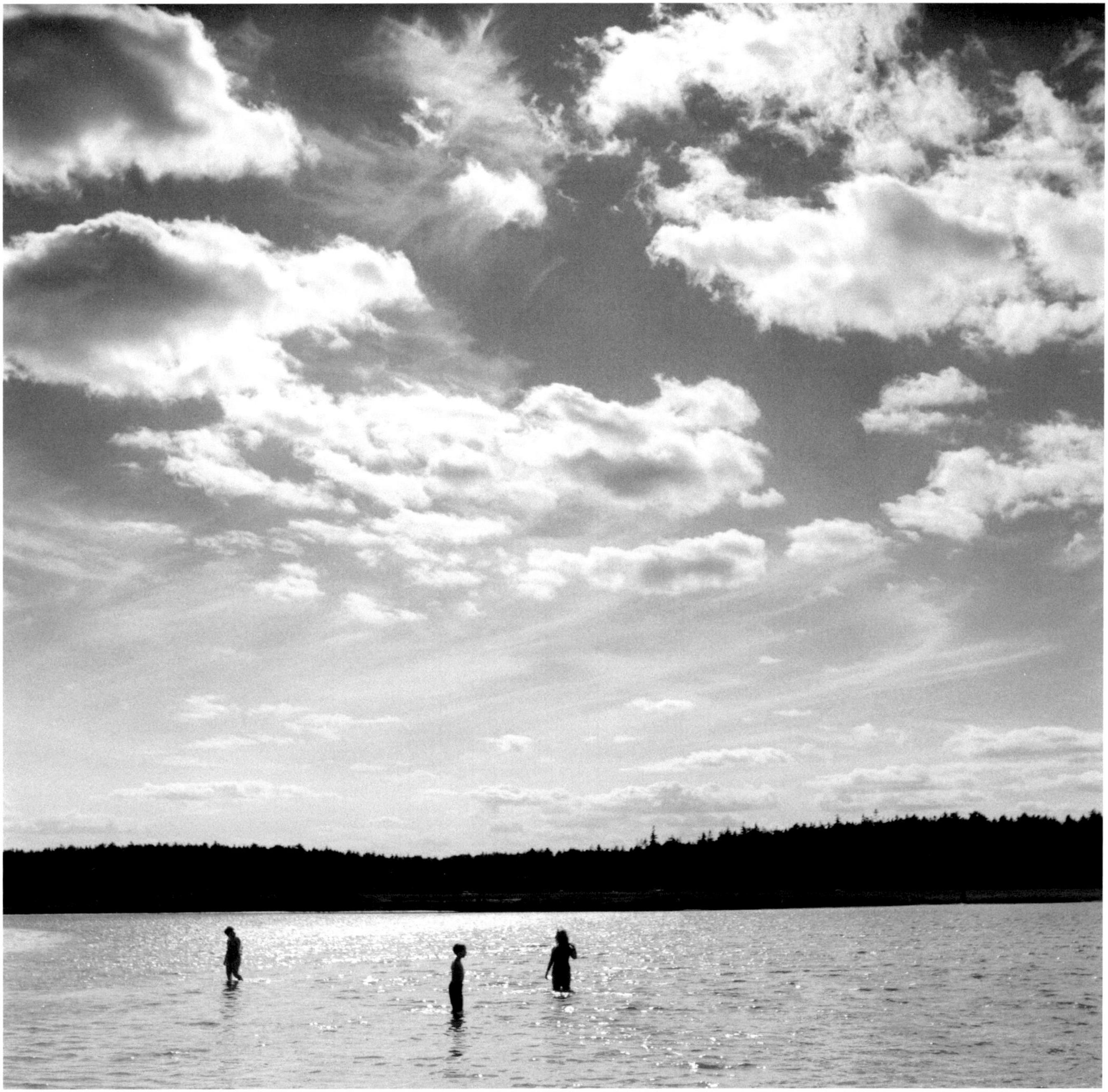

Popham Beach, 2003

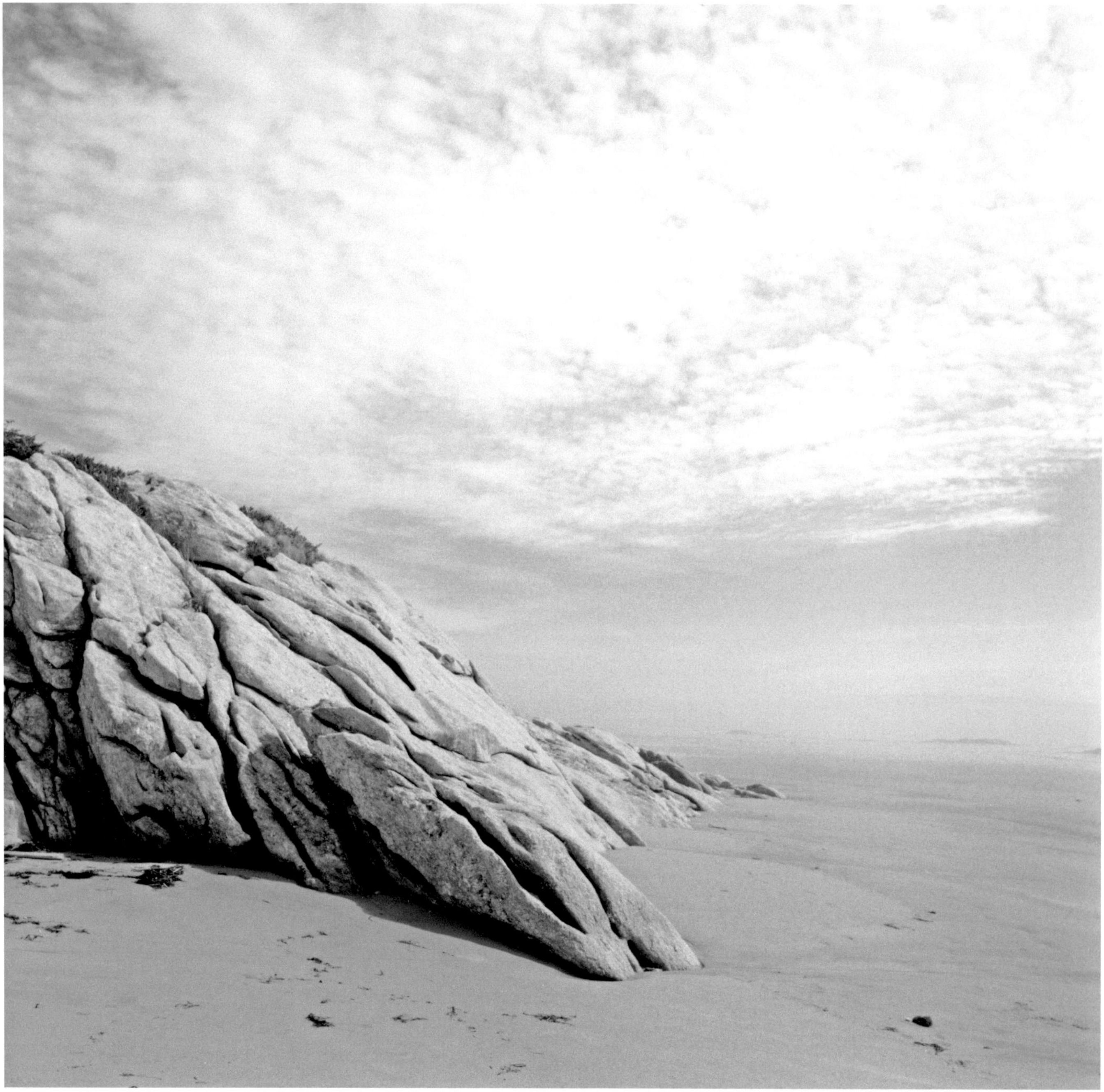

Morse Mountain, 2012

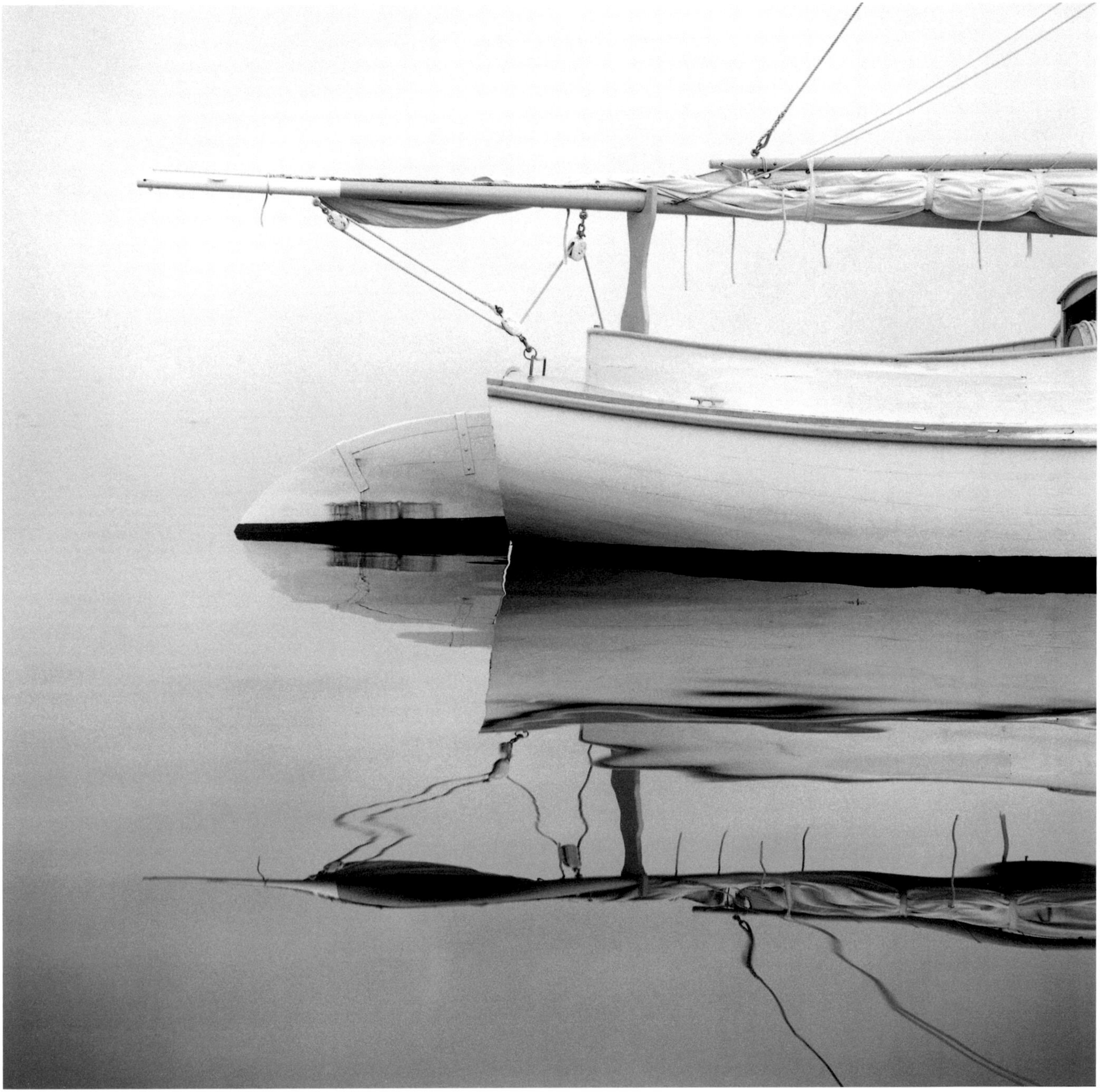

Brooklin, 2003

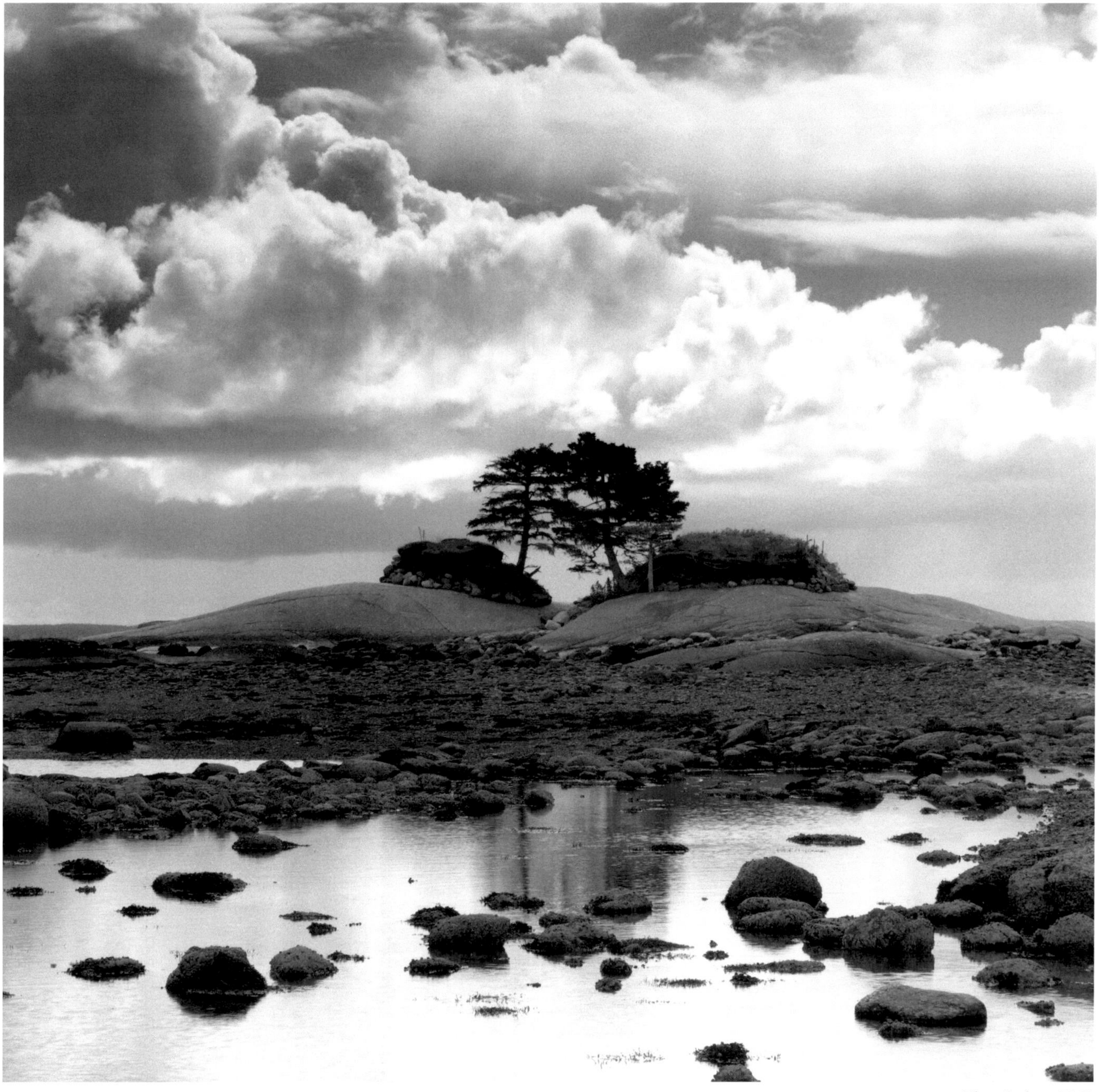
Flye Point, 2021

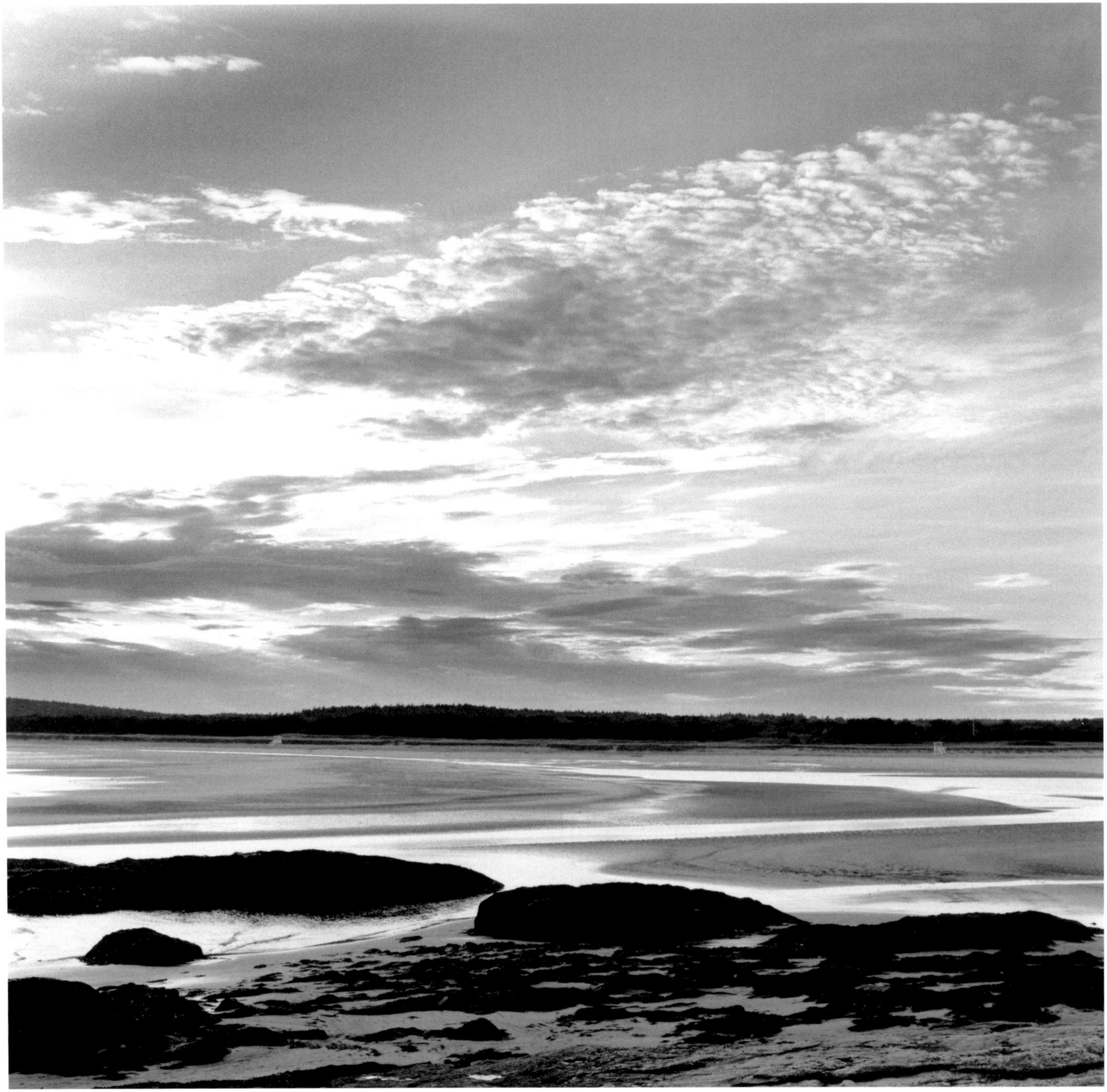

Phippsburg, 2002

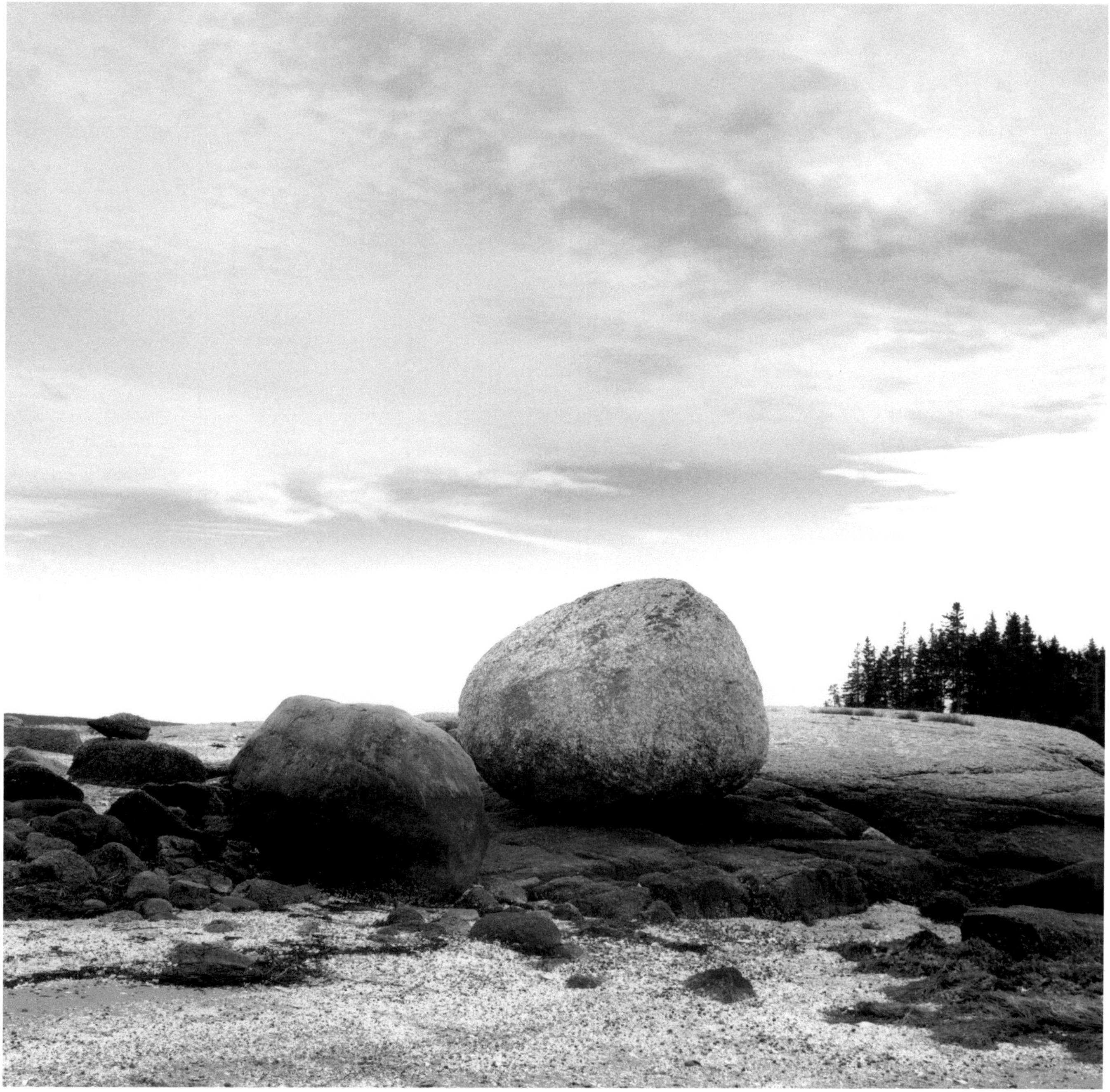

Eggemogin Reach, 2021

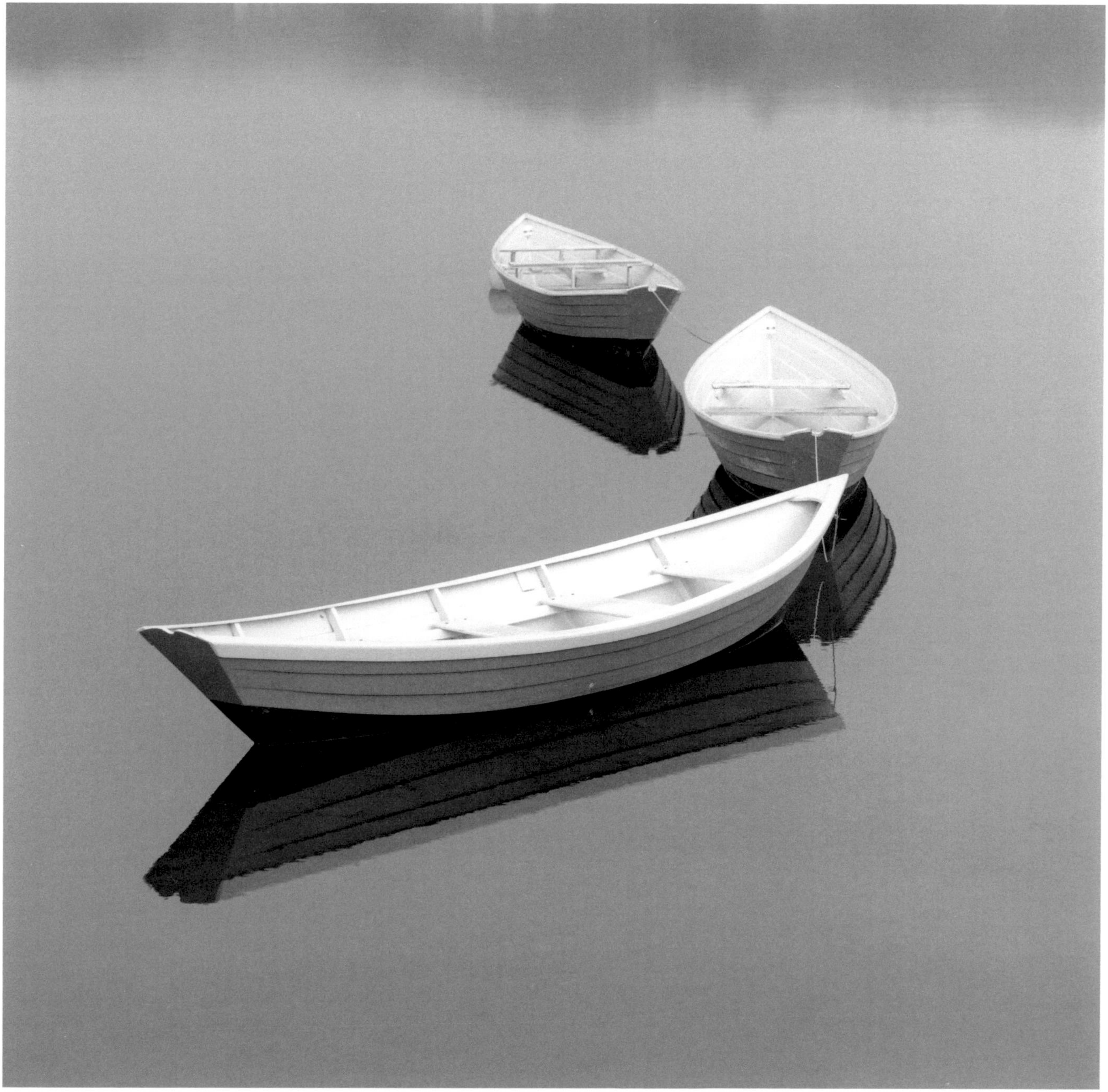

Kennebunkport, 2011

We do not need time or money to enjoy the wind or the stars or the rain or the thousand other constantly changing events that surround our lives, but what we must have is awareness and curiosity.

—ROY BARRETTE

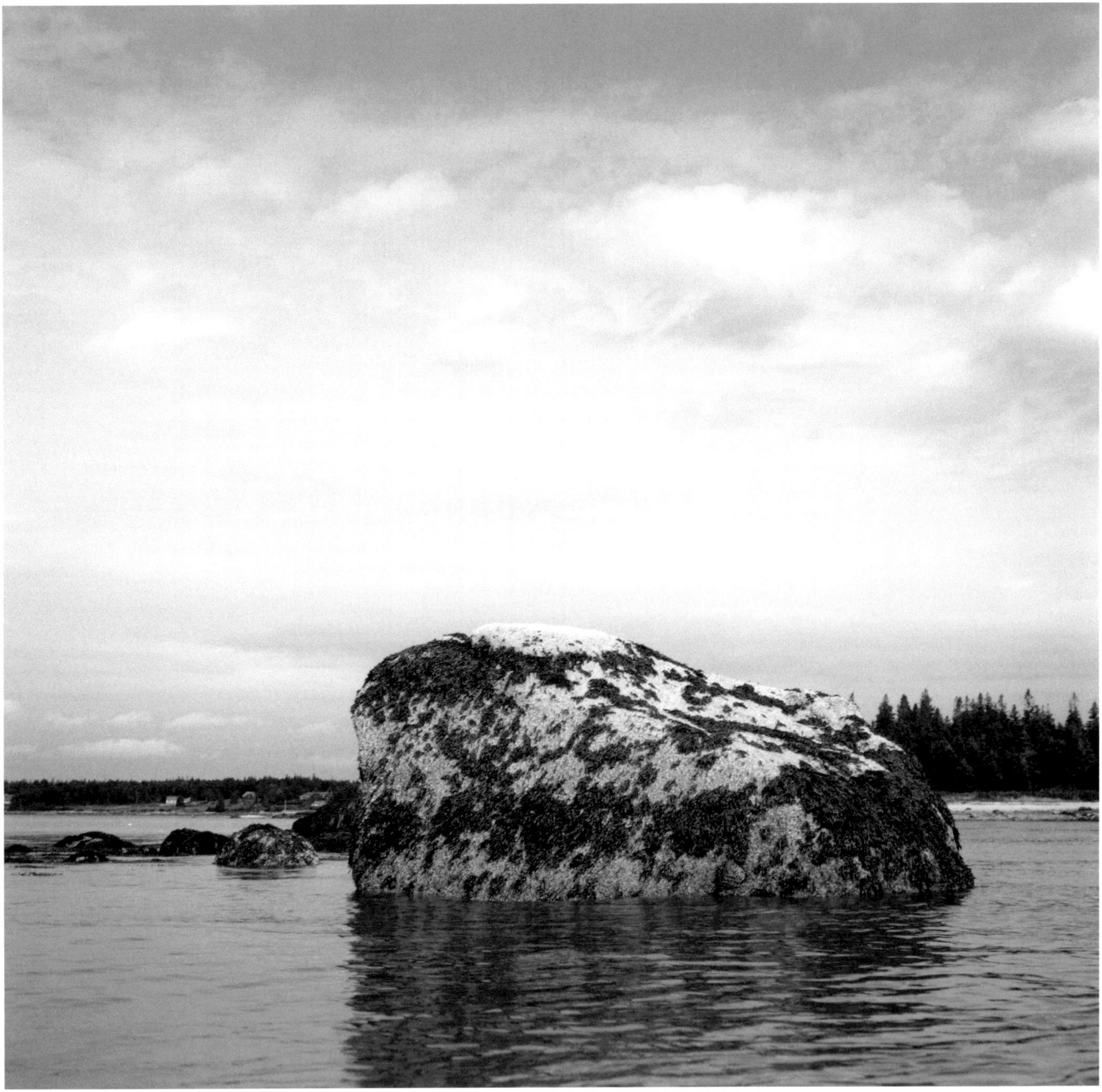
Sellers Island, 2022

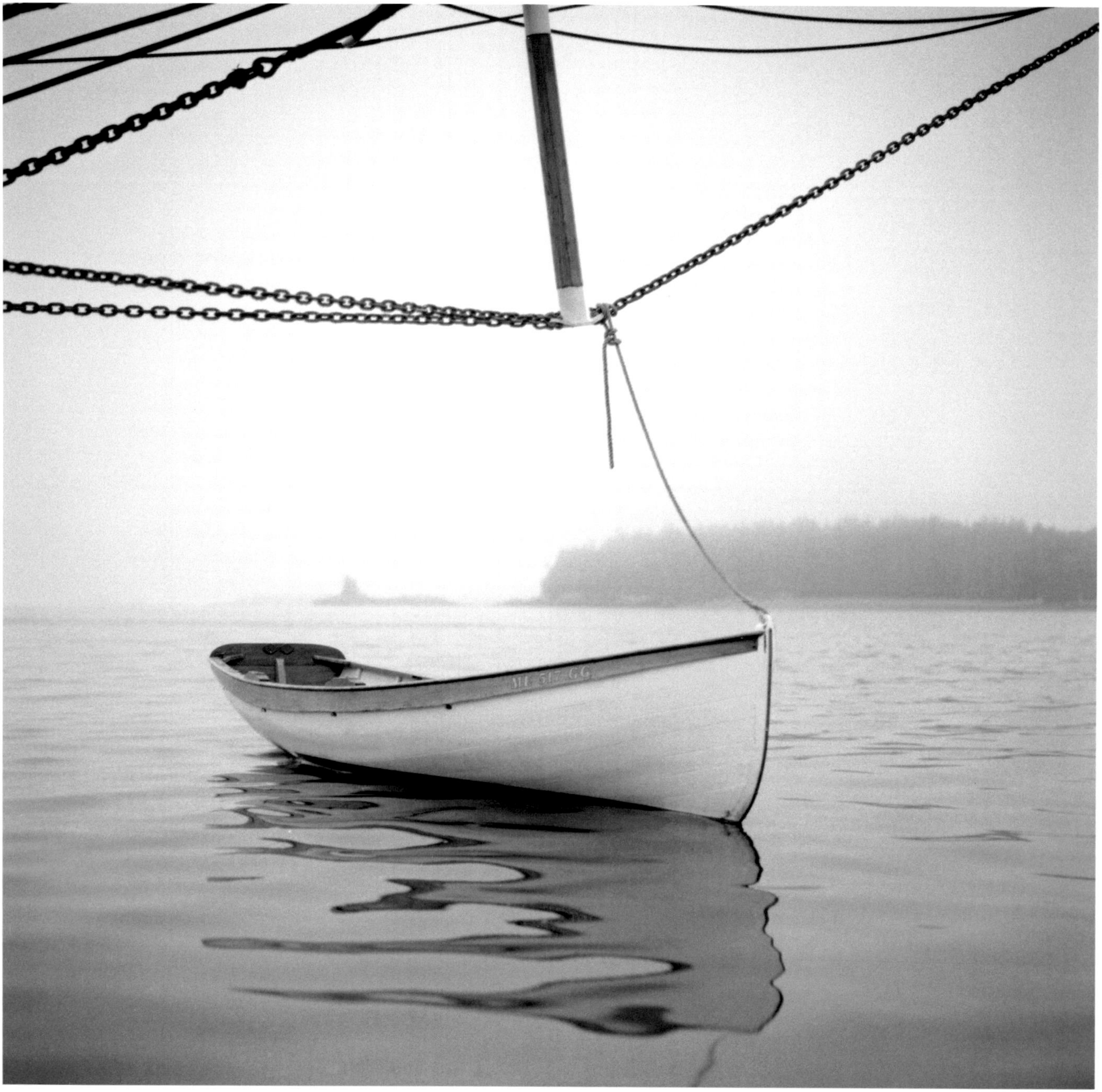

Great Cove, 1999

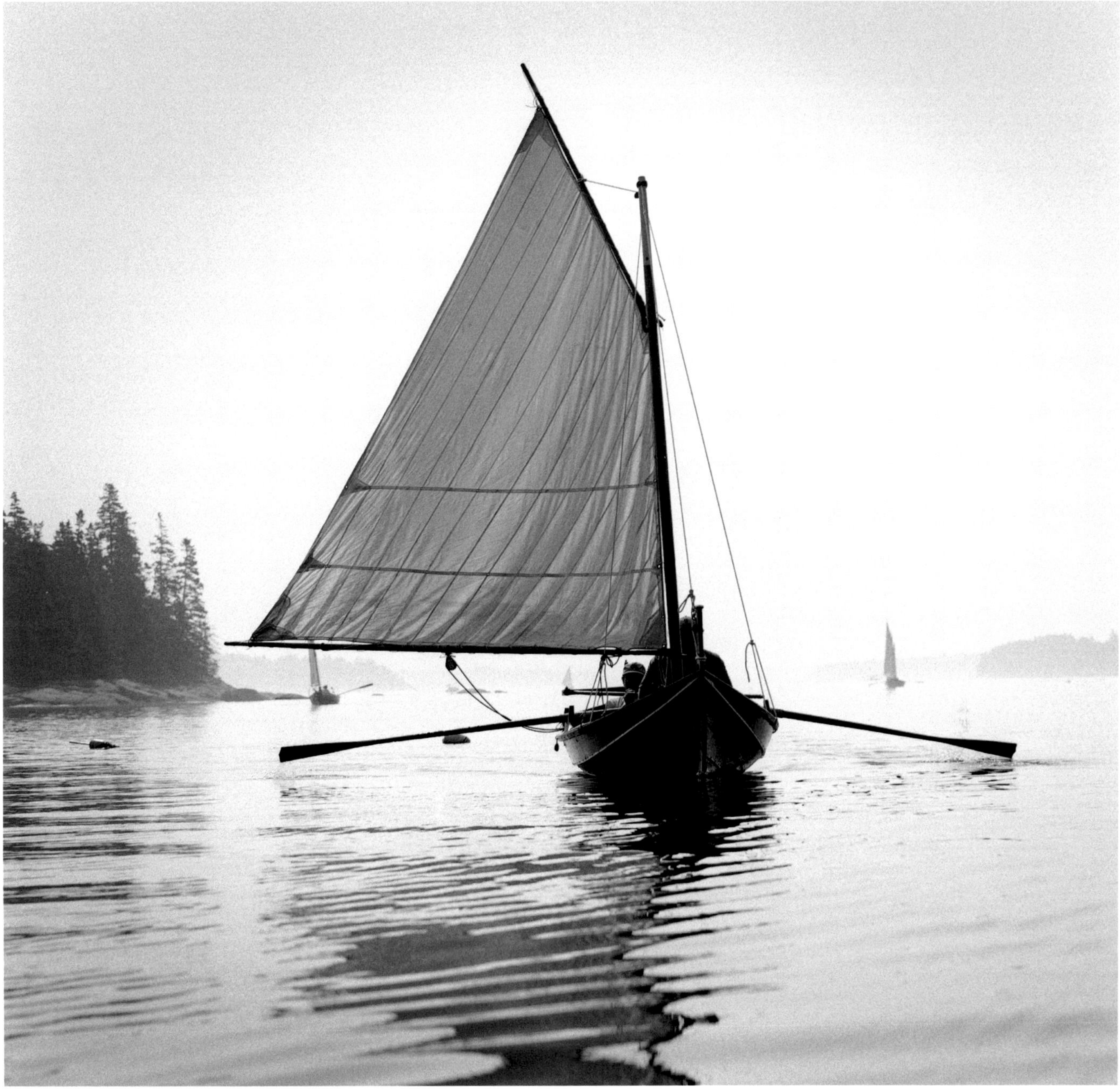

Center Harbor, 2007

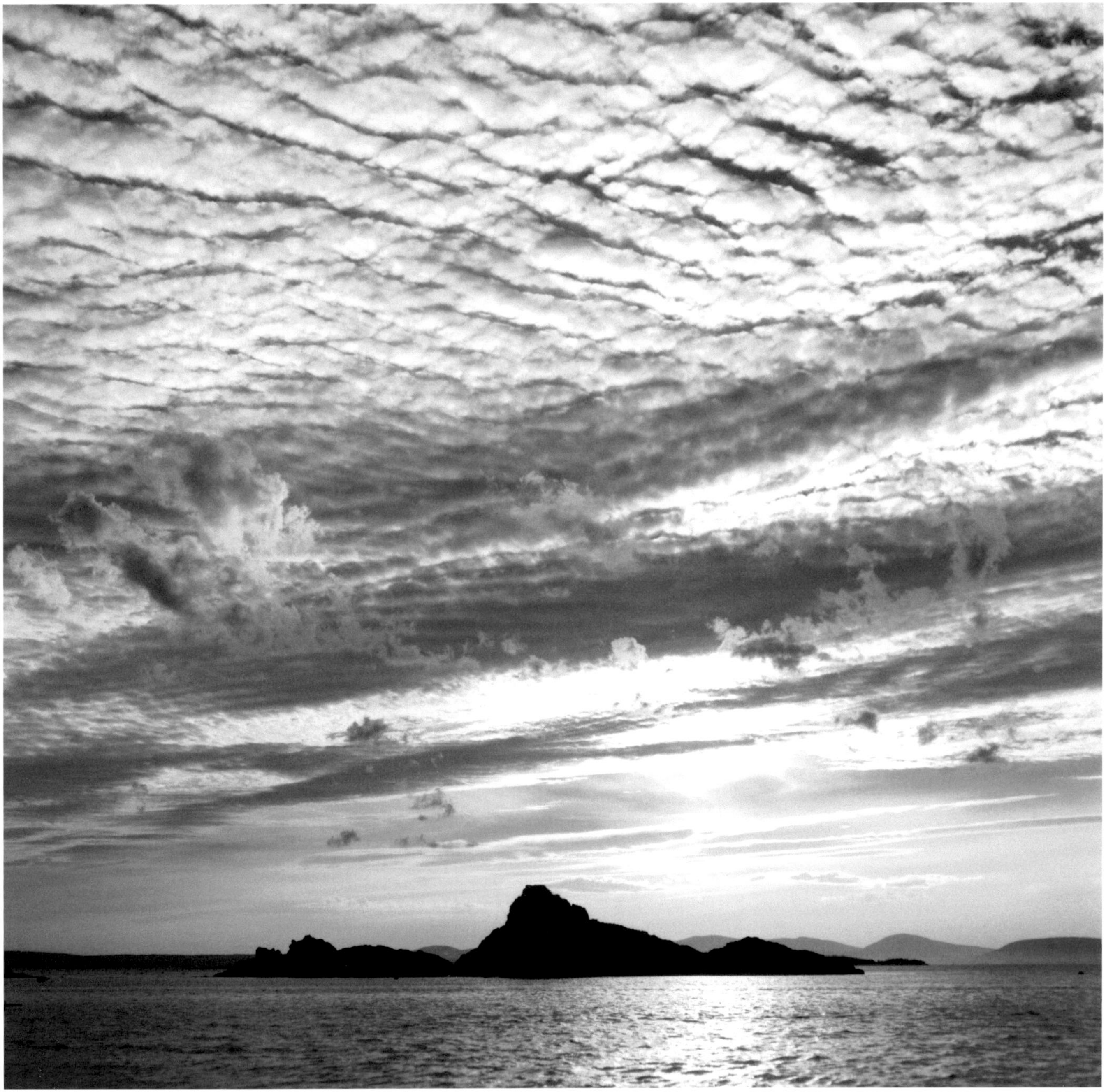

Pulpit Harbor, 2004

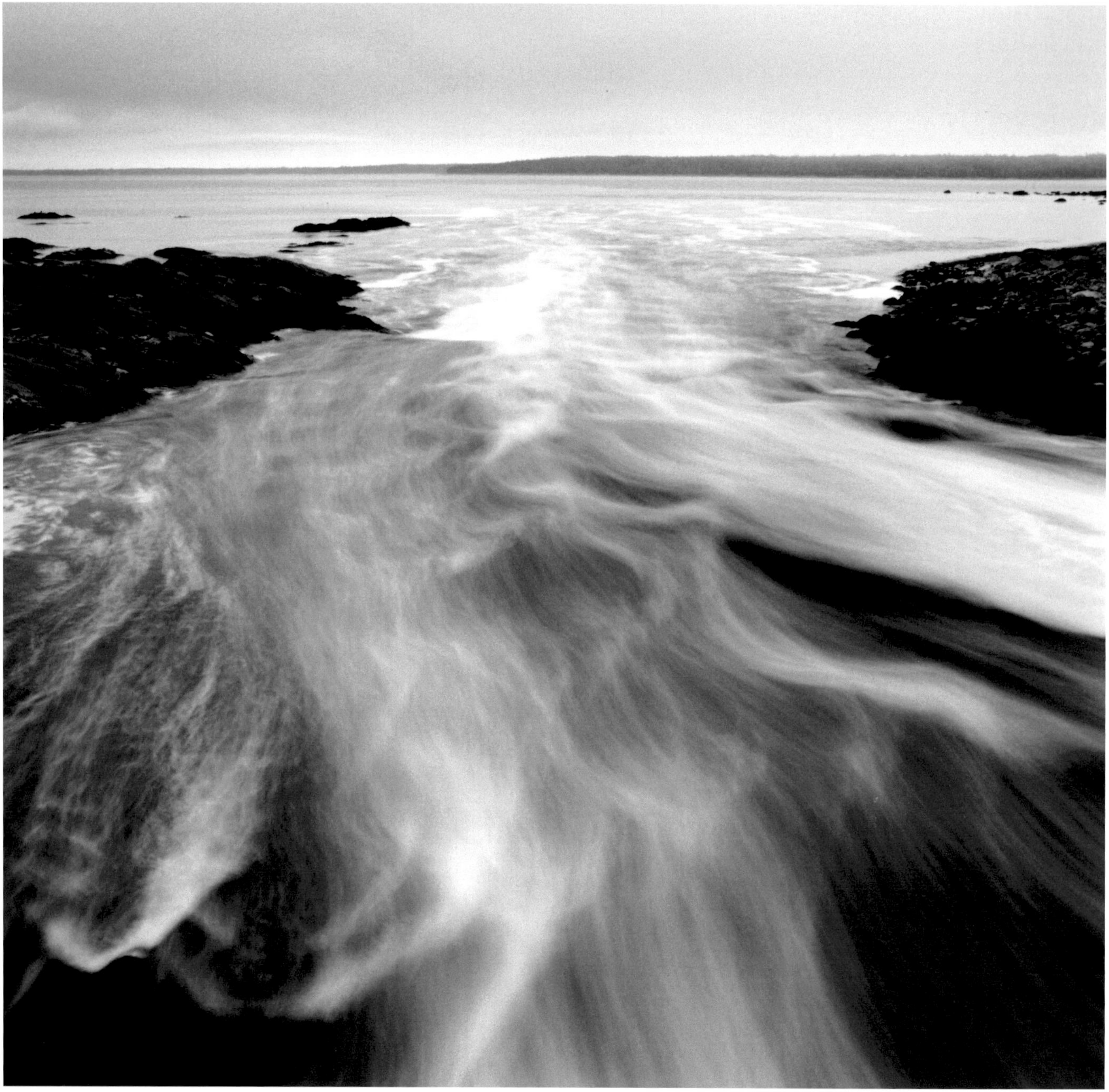

Blue Hill, 2019

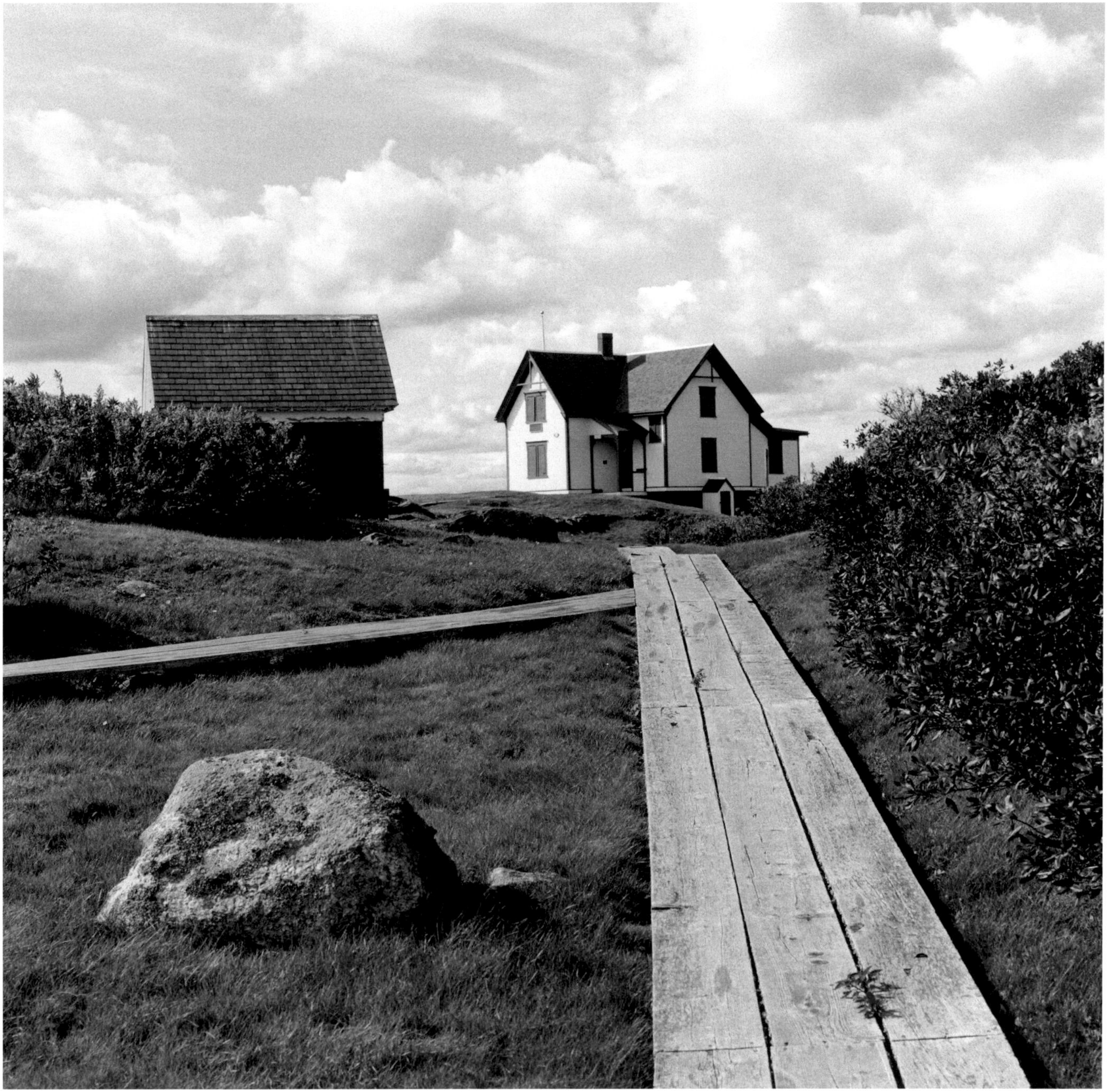

Ram Island, 2009

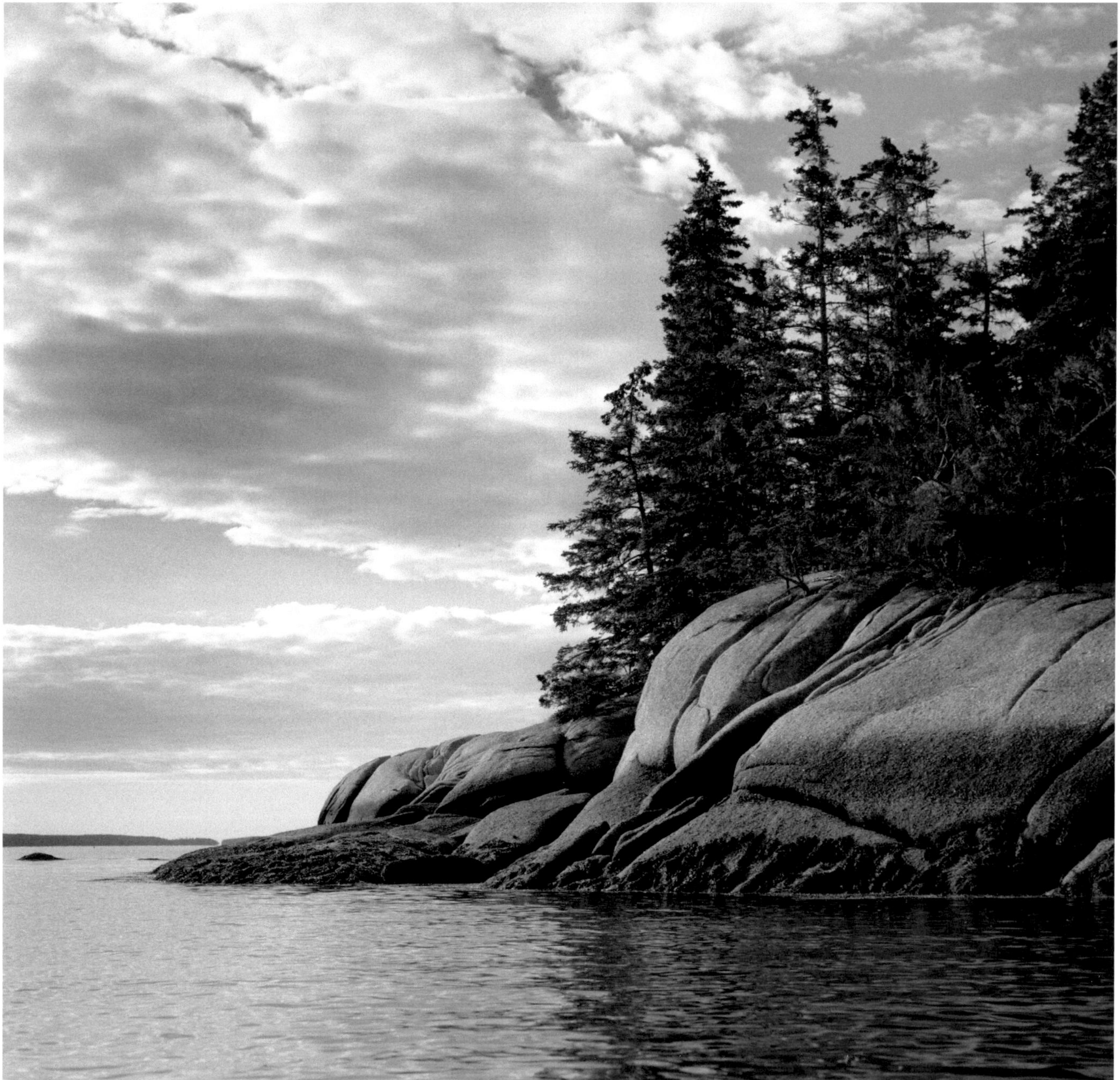

Hog Island, 2022

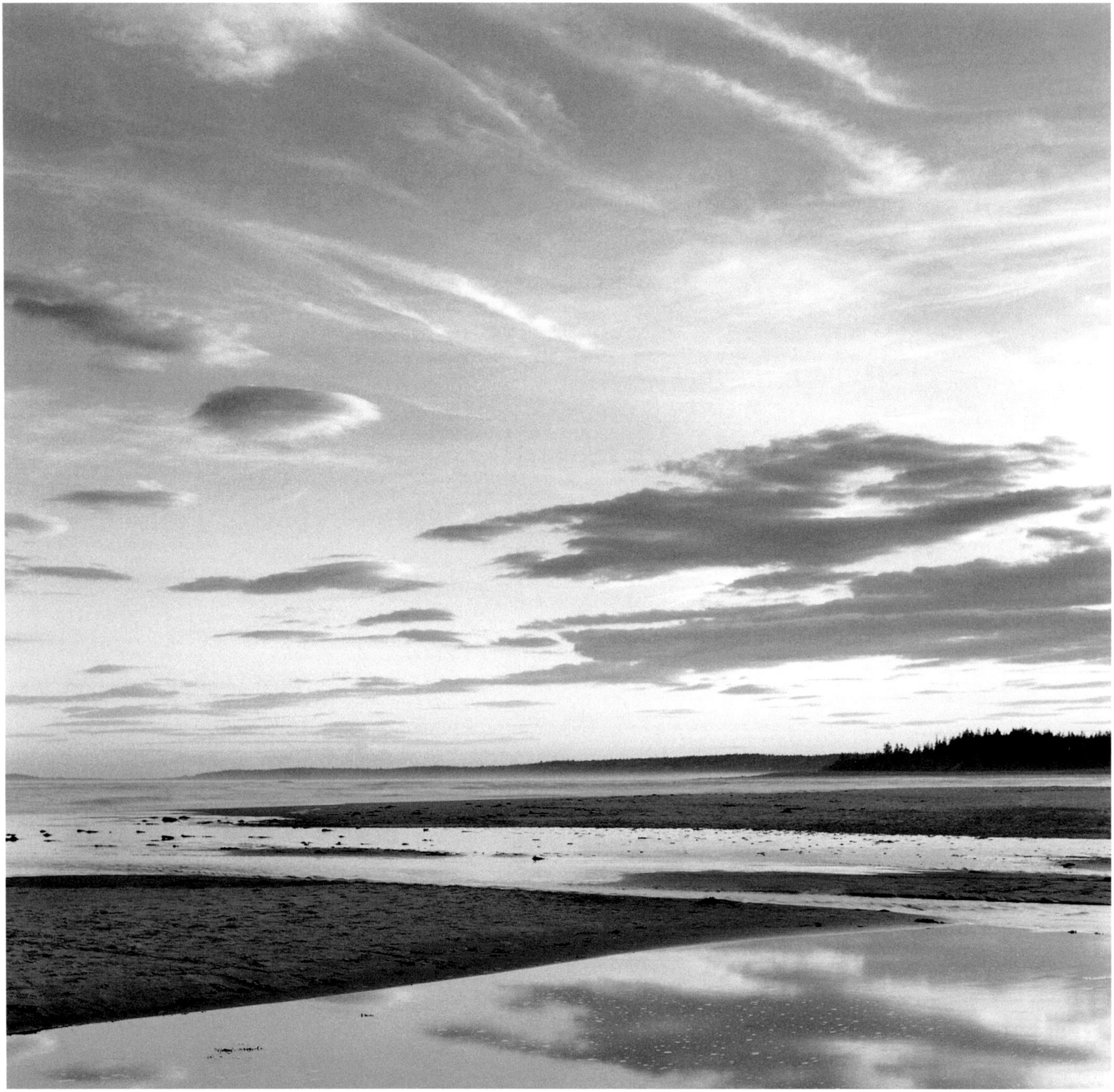

Popham Beach, 2000

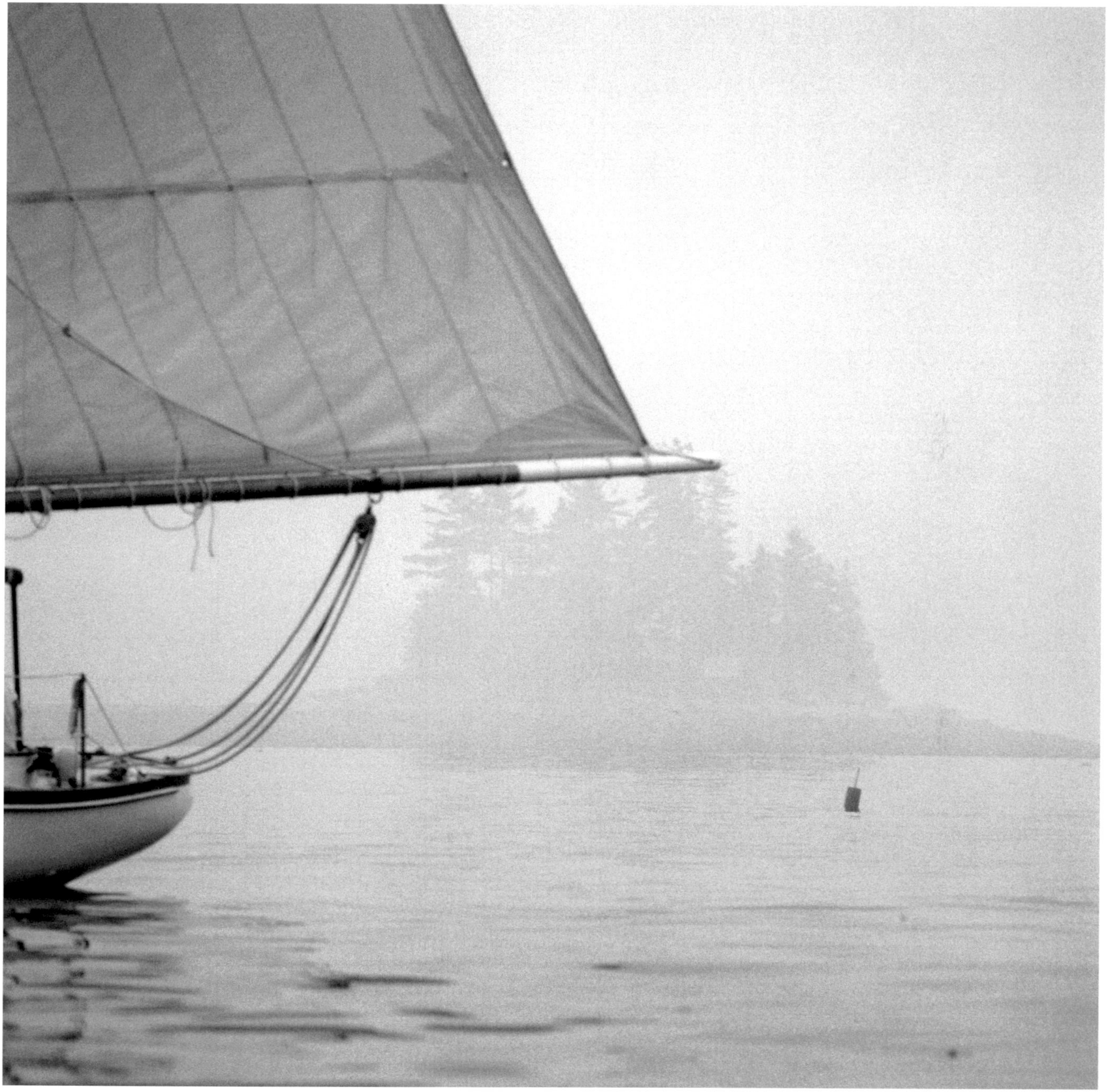

Gulf of Maine, 2003

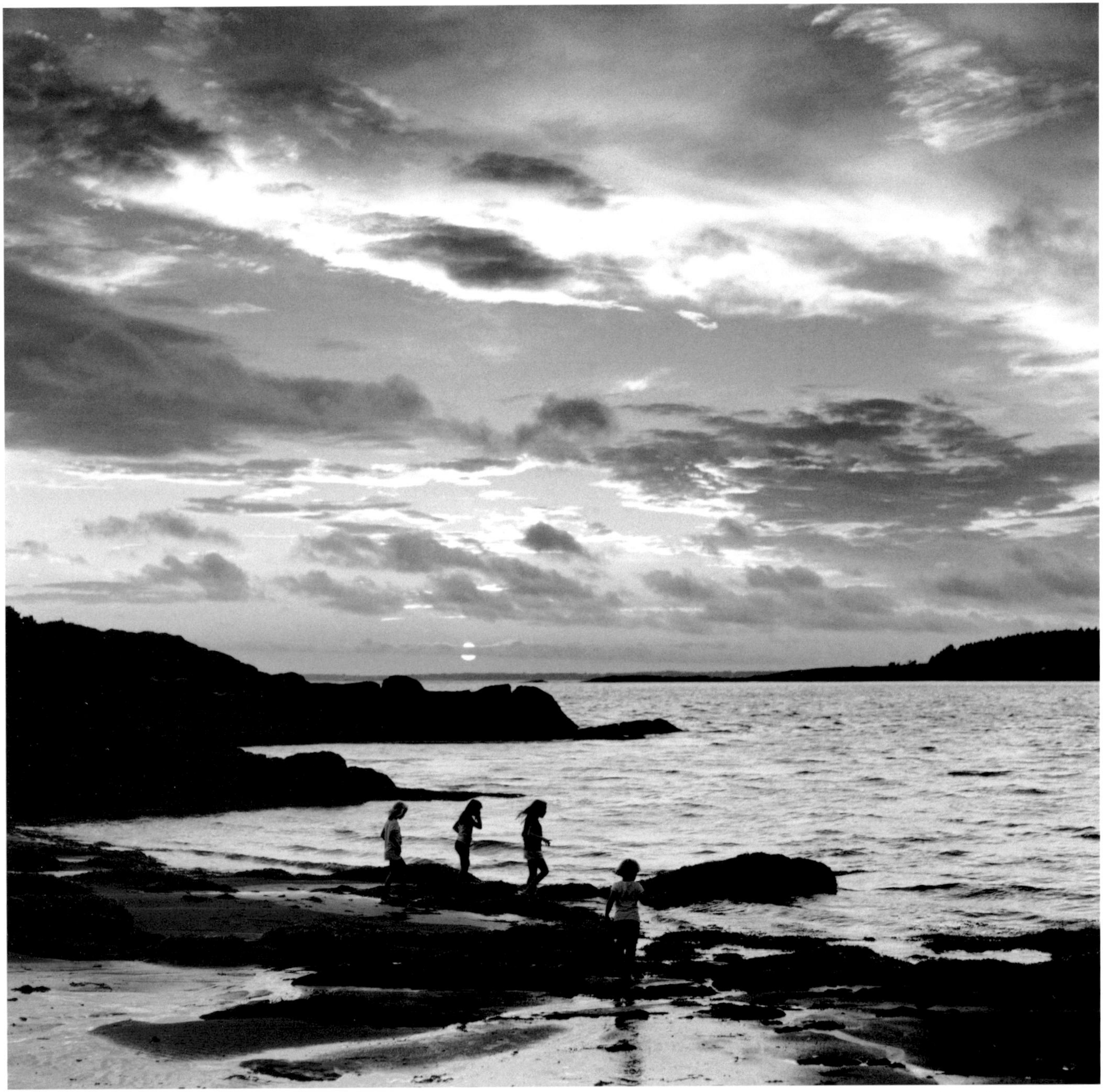

Hermit Island, 2012

You have to knock a few times
before the harbor will let you in.

—MICHAEL KAHN ON SAILING
A SMALL BOAT IN MAINE

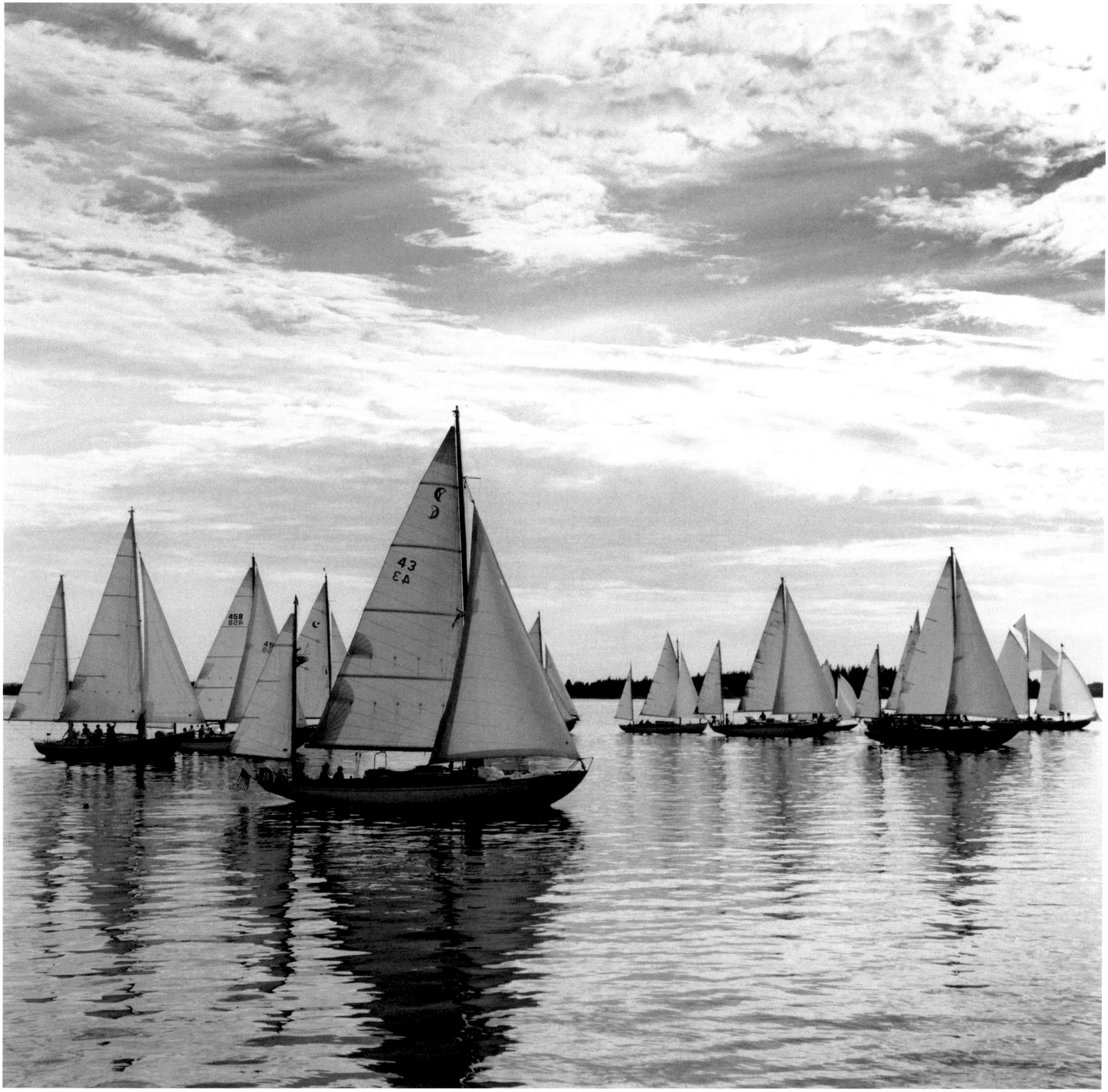

Great Cove, 2004

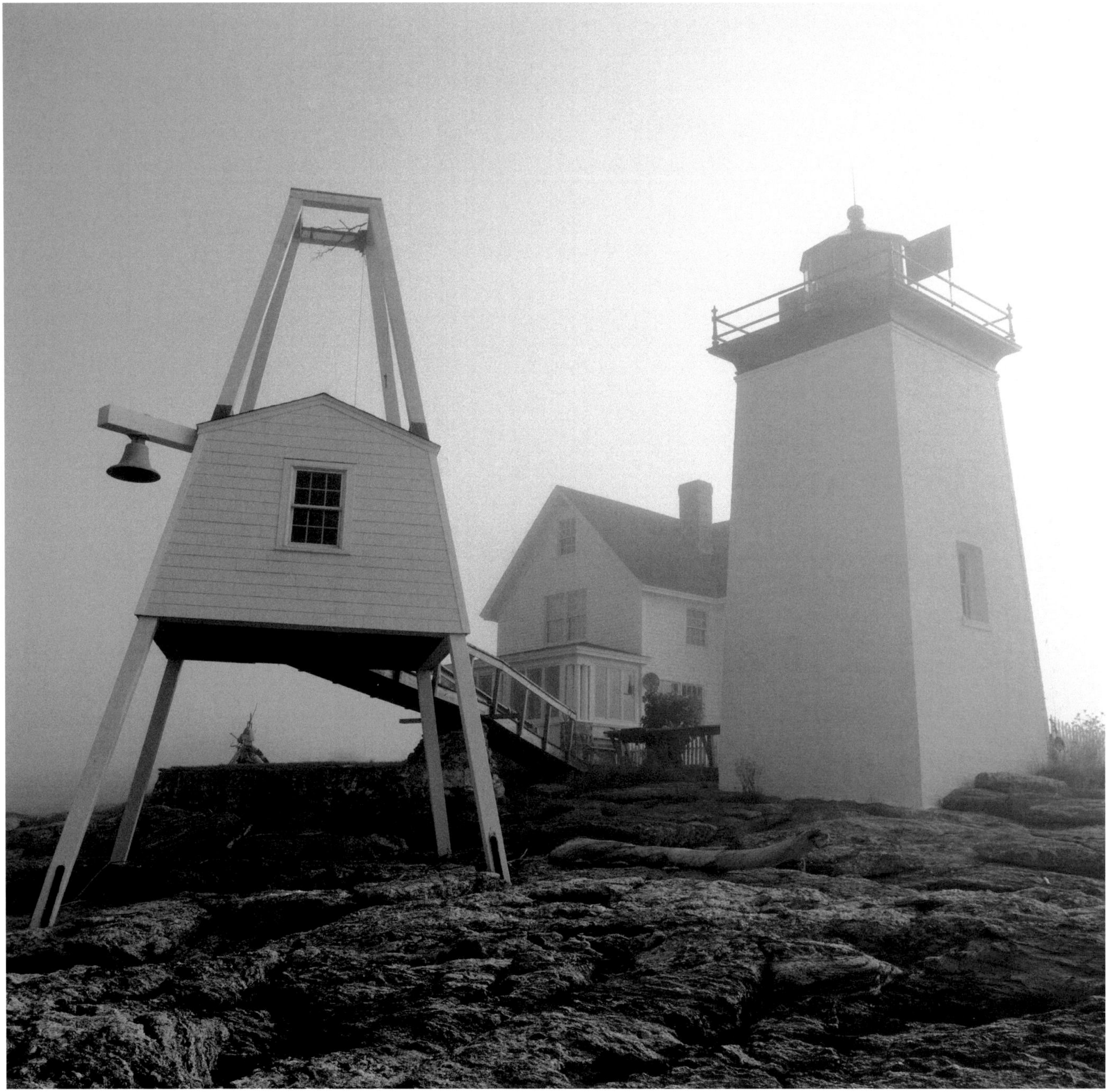

Hendrick's Head Lighthouse, 2005

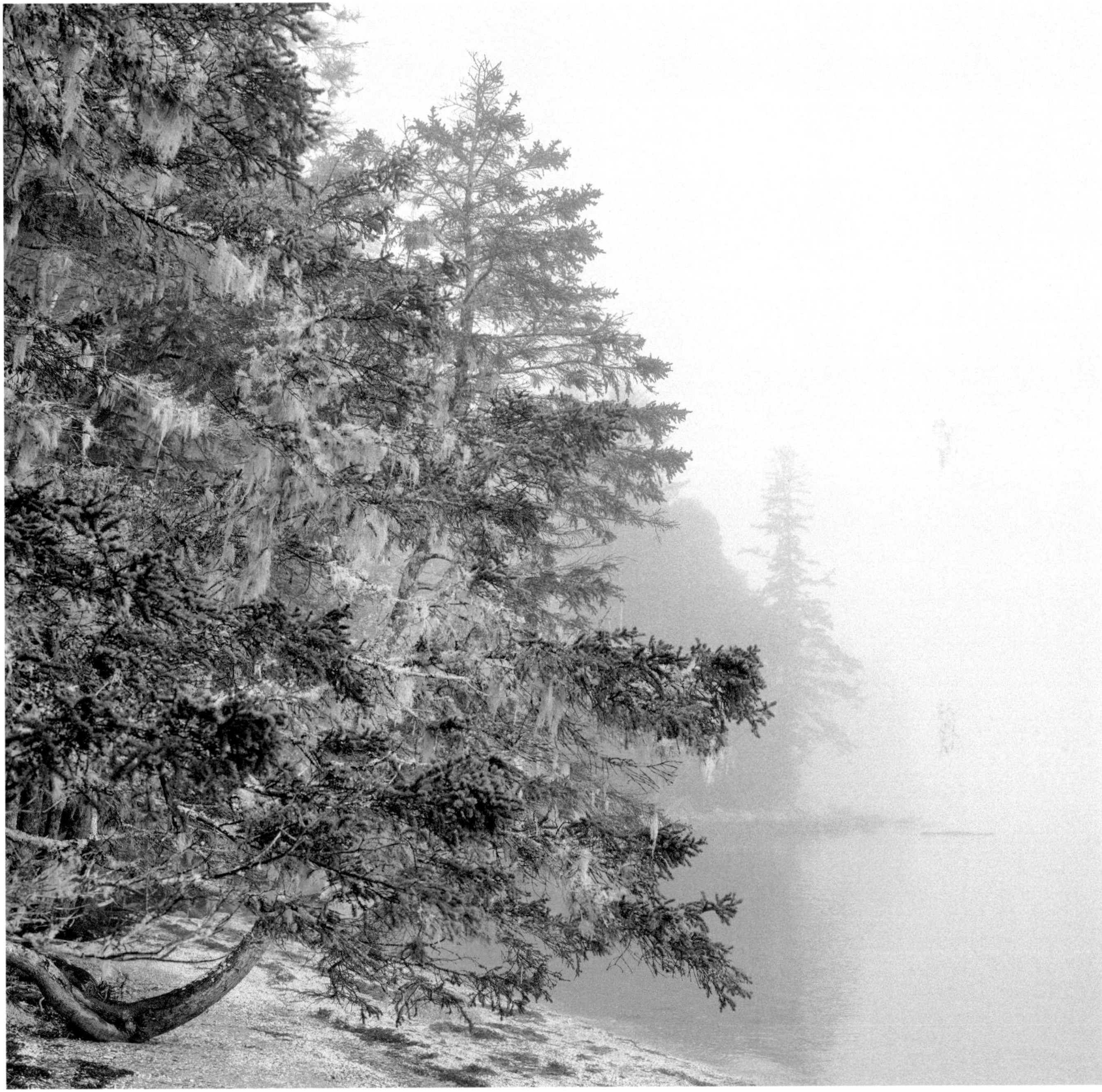

Babson Island, 2021

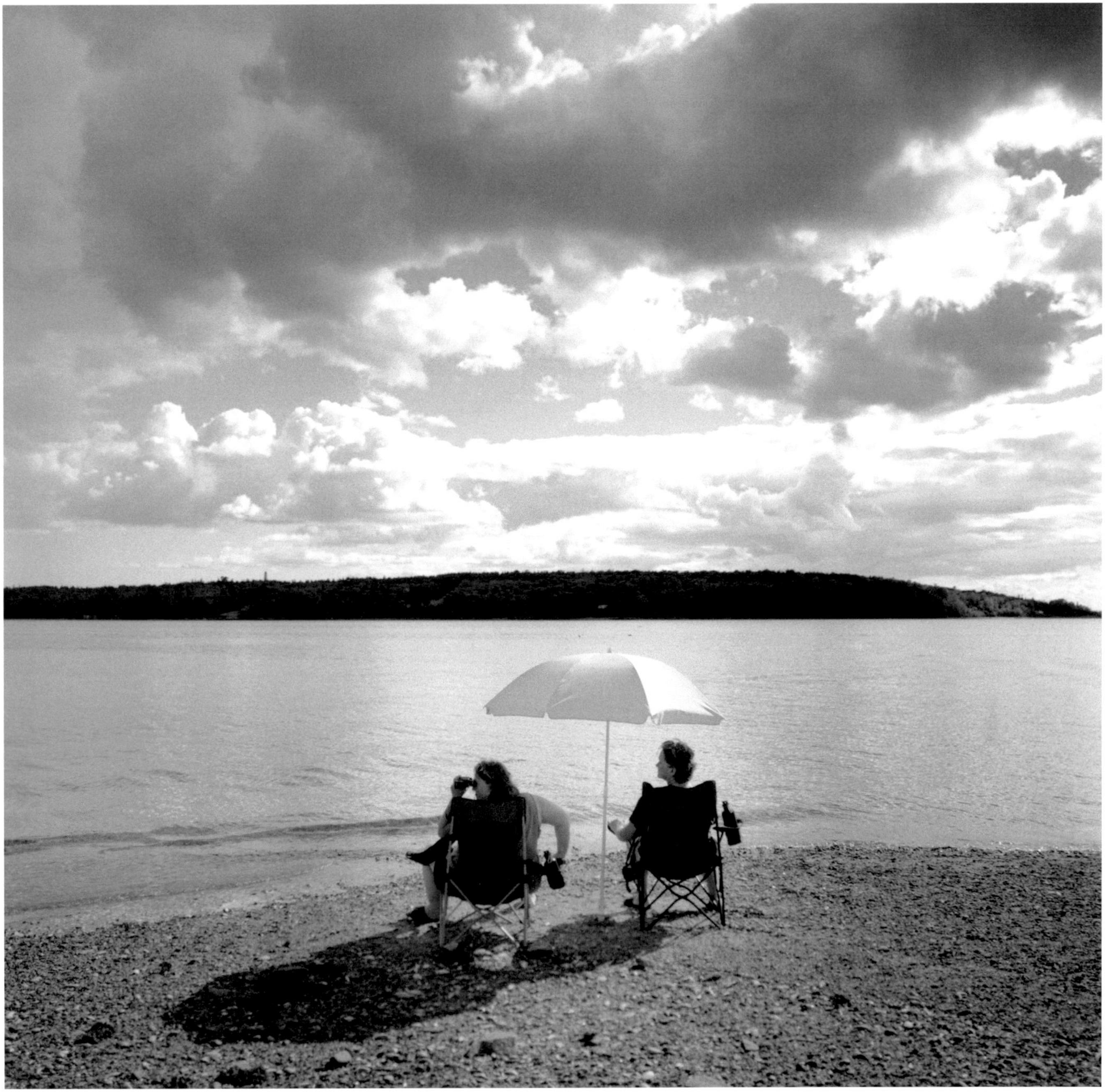

Lamoine State Park, 2011

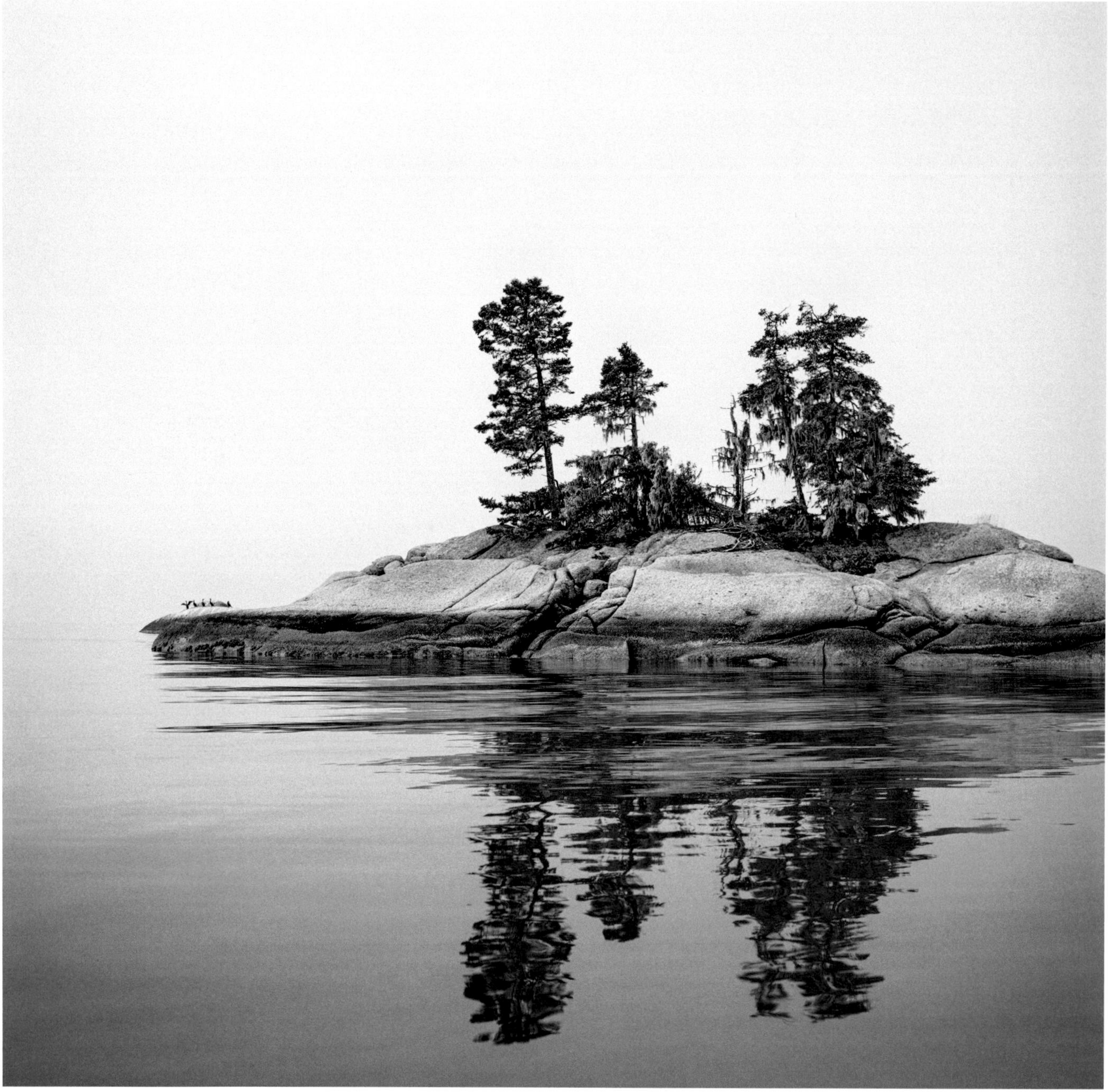

Eggemogin Reach, 2022

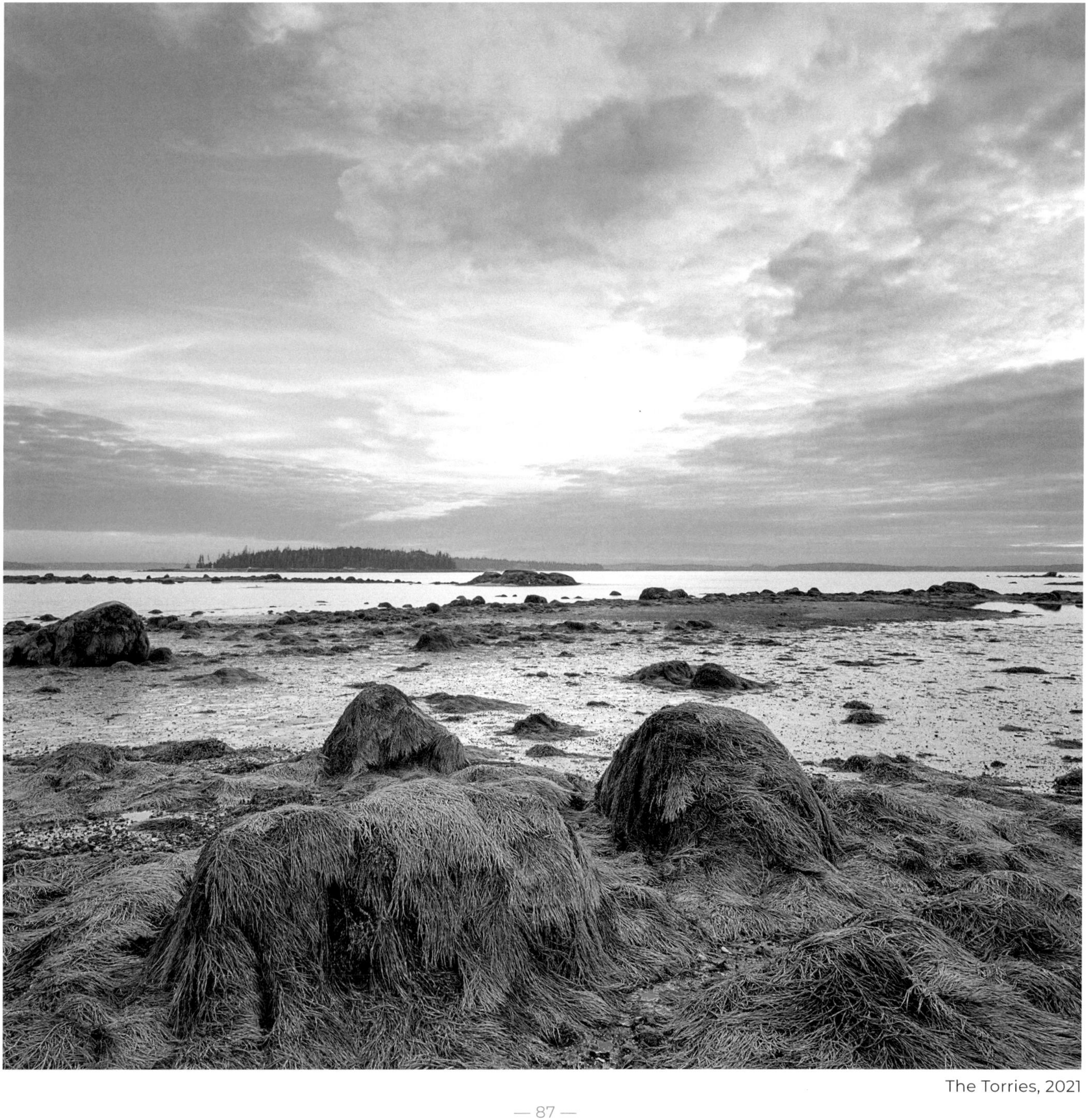

The Torries, 2021

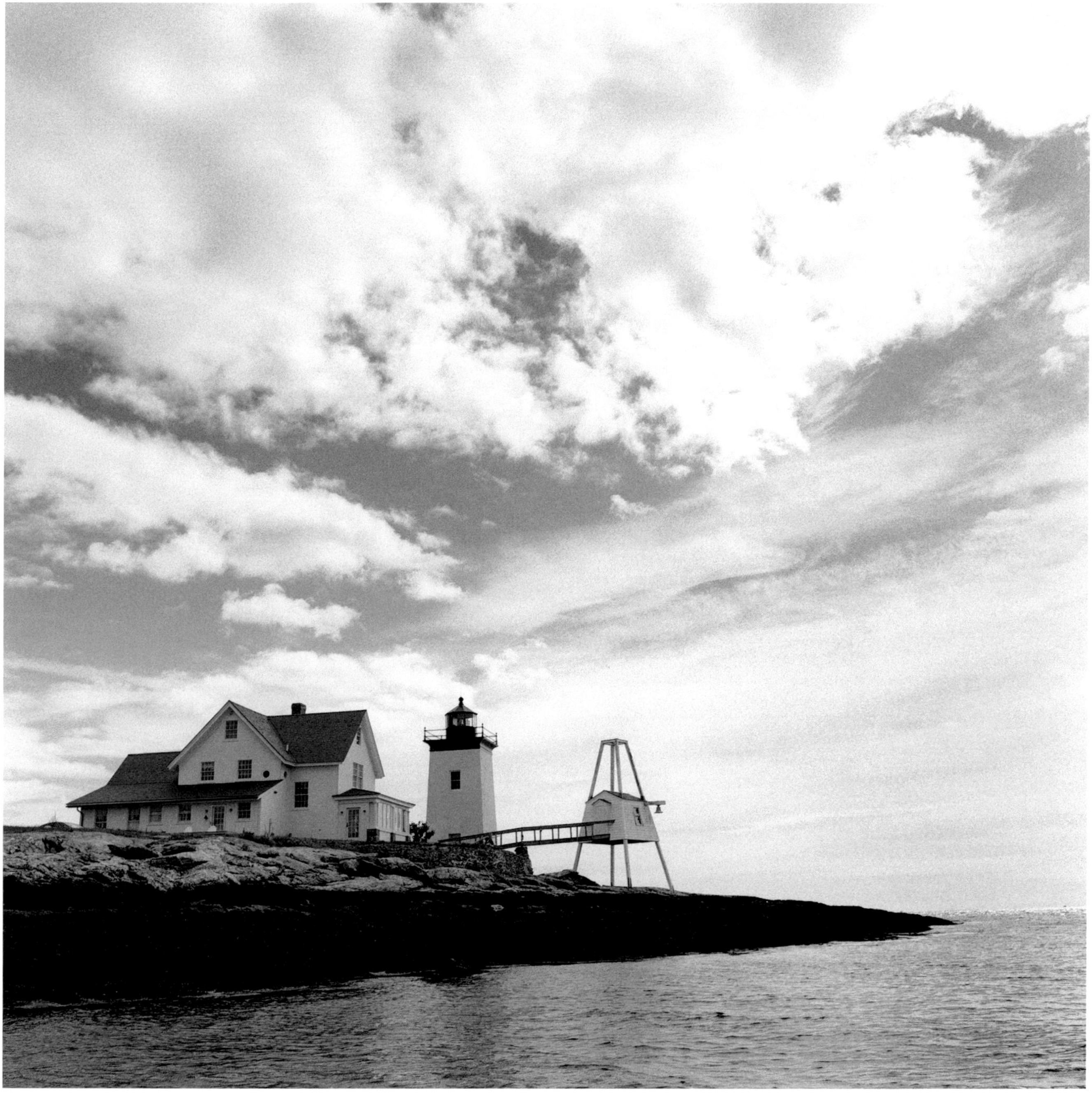
Southport, 2009

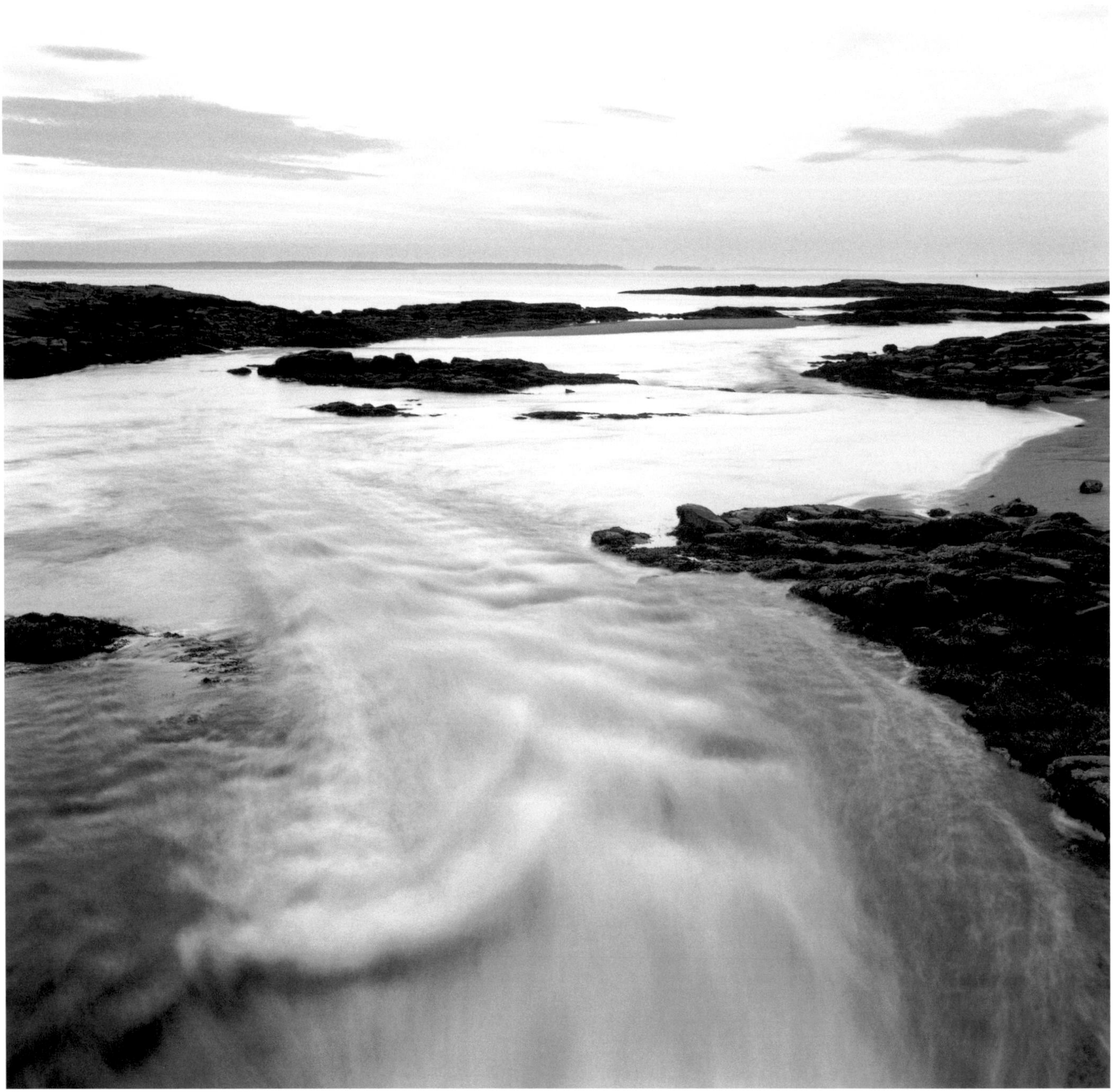

Reid State Park, 2002

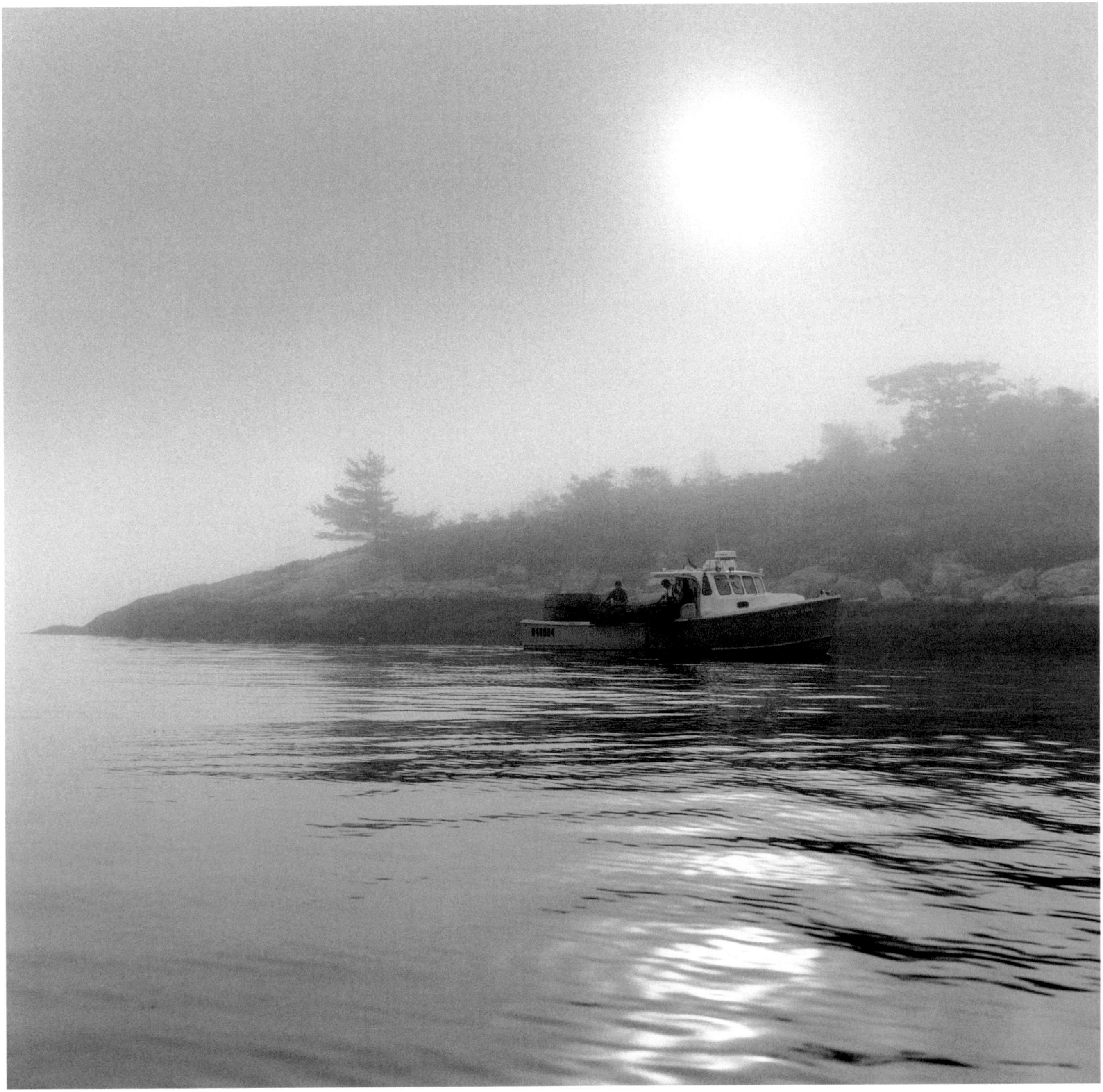

Gulf of Maine, 2005

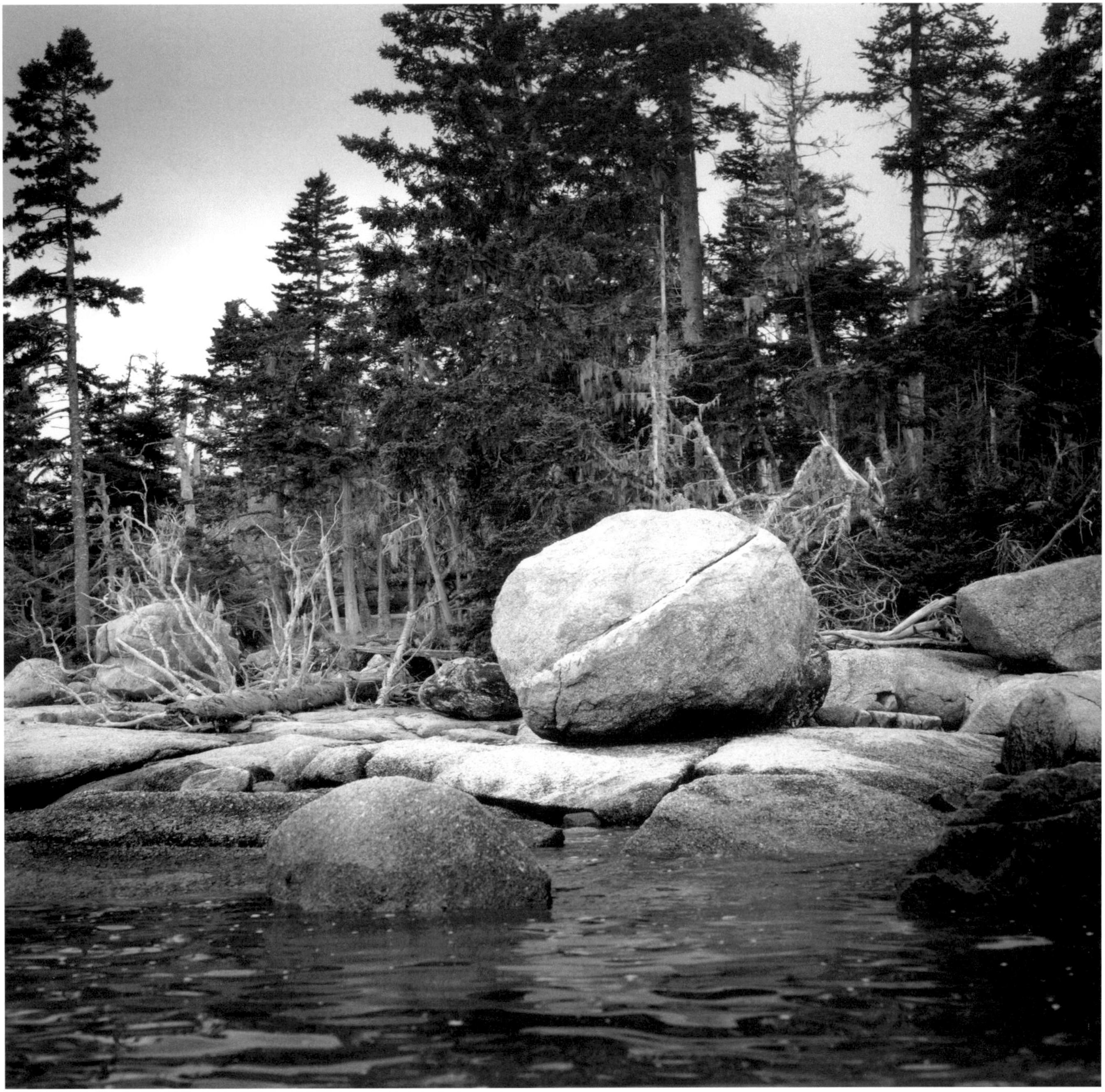

Harbor Island, 2022

Life's meaning has always eluded me and I guess it always will.
But I love it just the same.

—E. B. WHITE

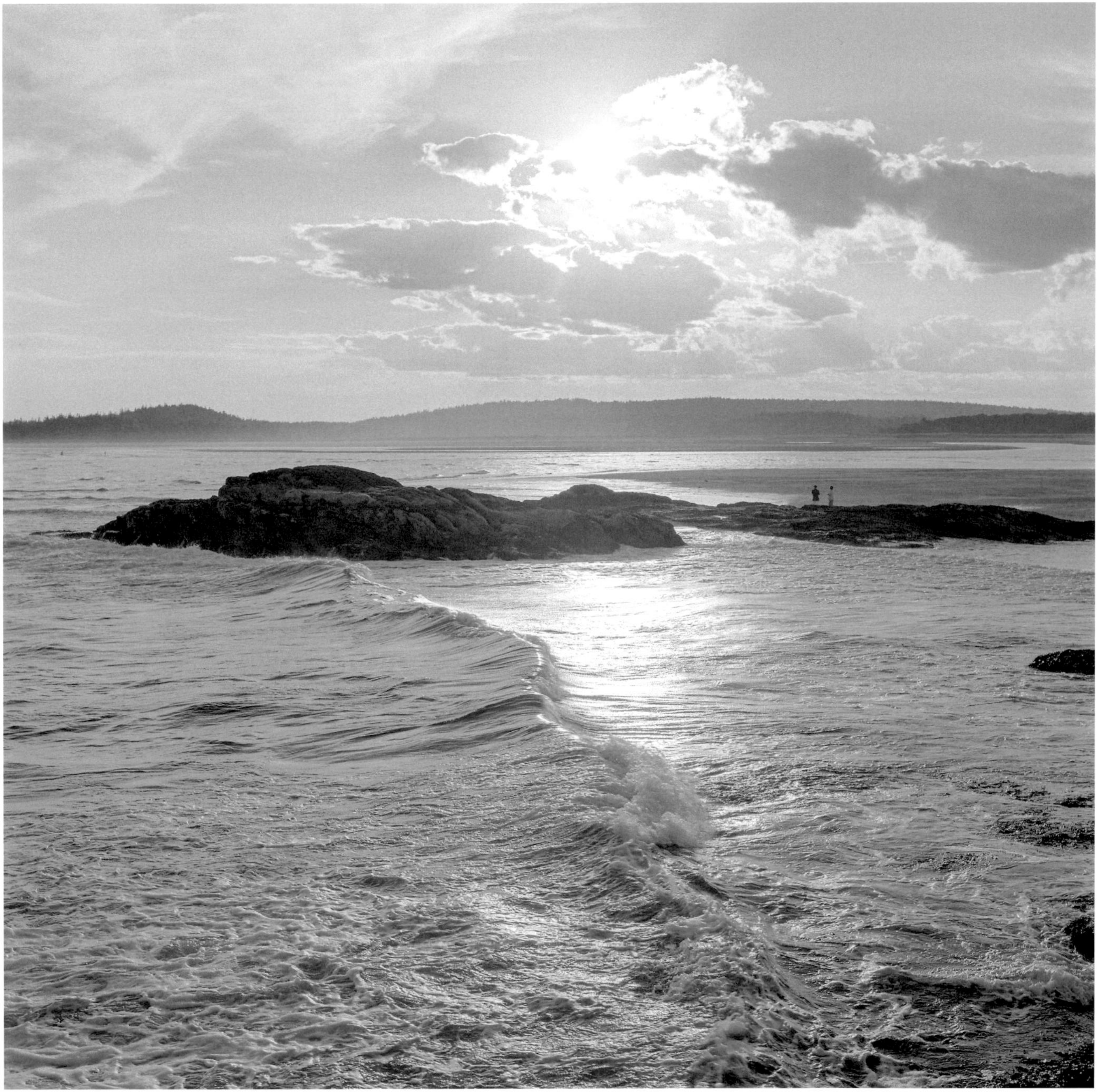

Popham Beach, 2006

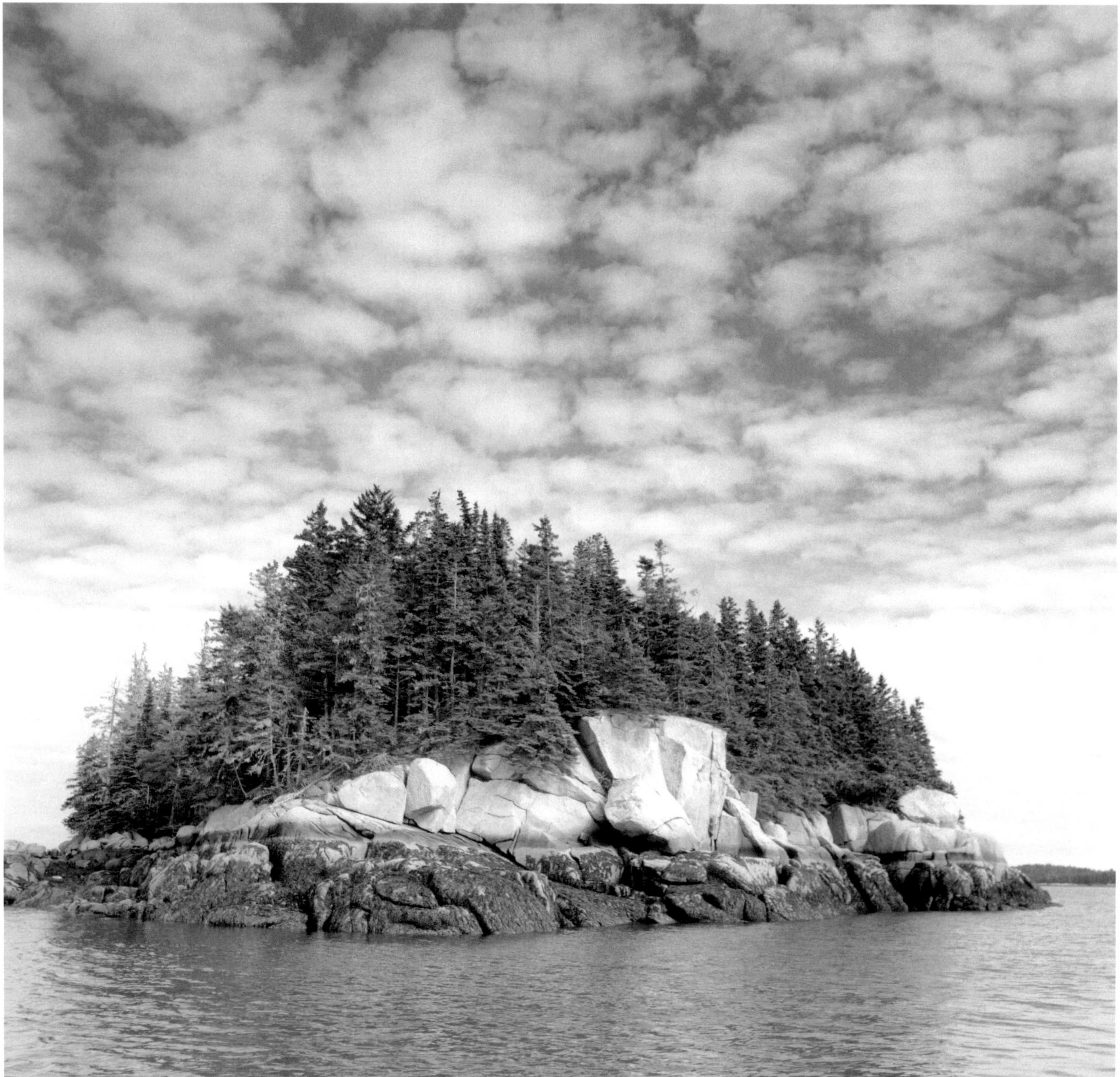

Sprout Island, 2022

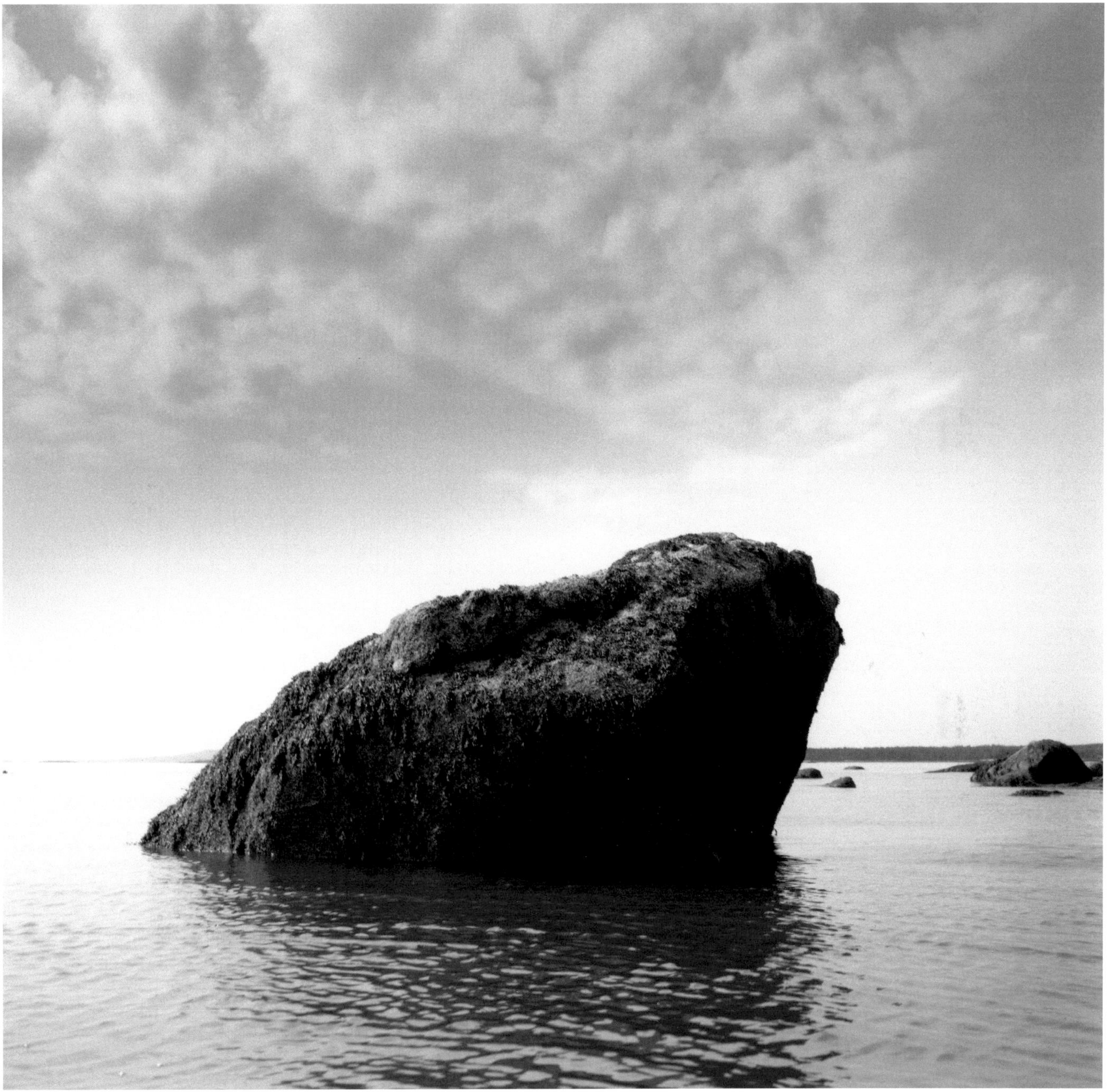

Jericho Bay, 2022

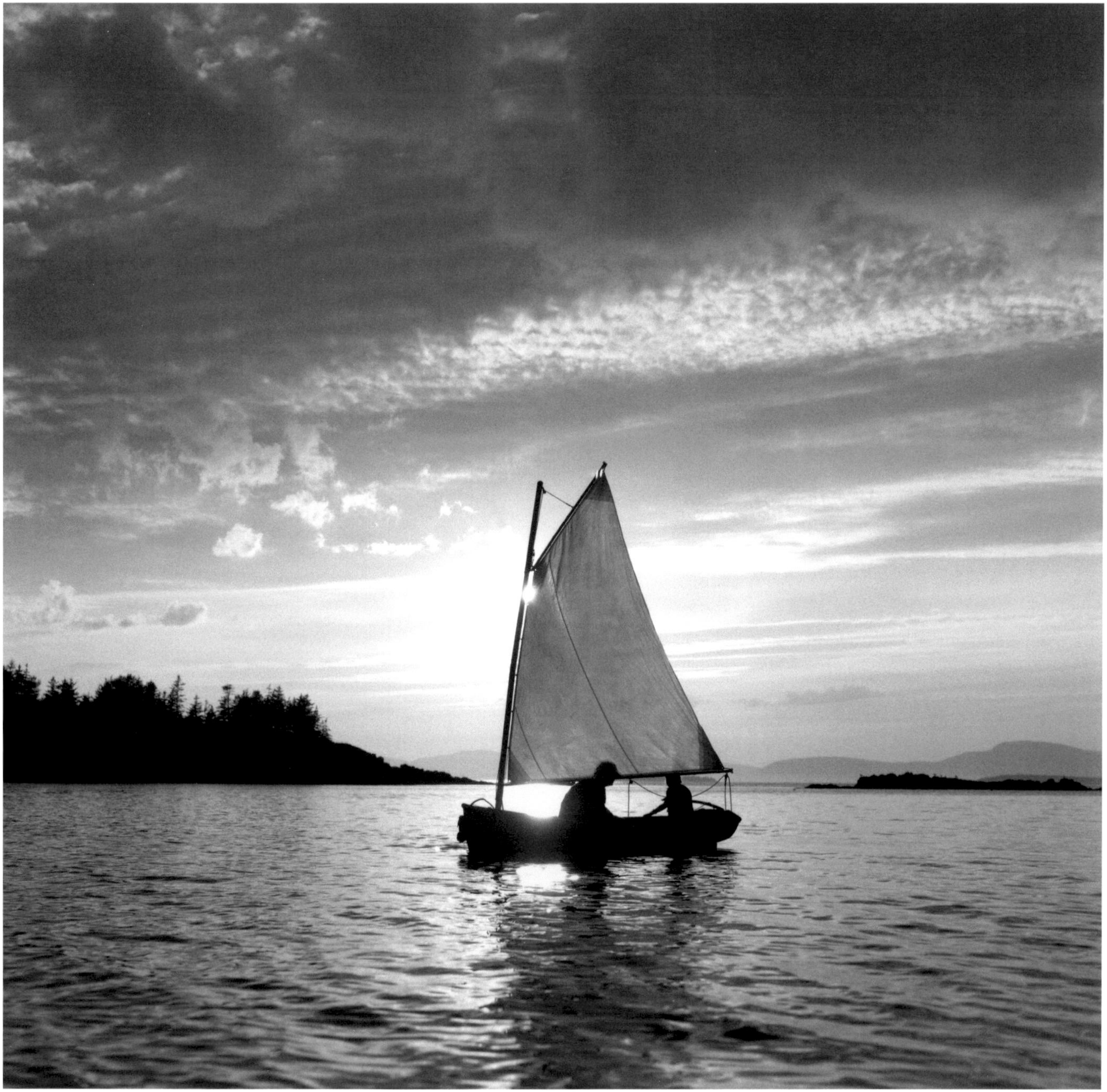

North Haven Island, 2004

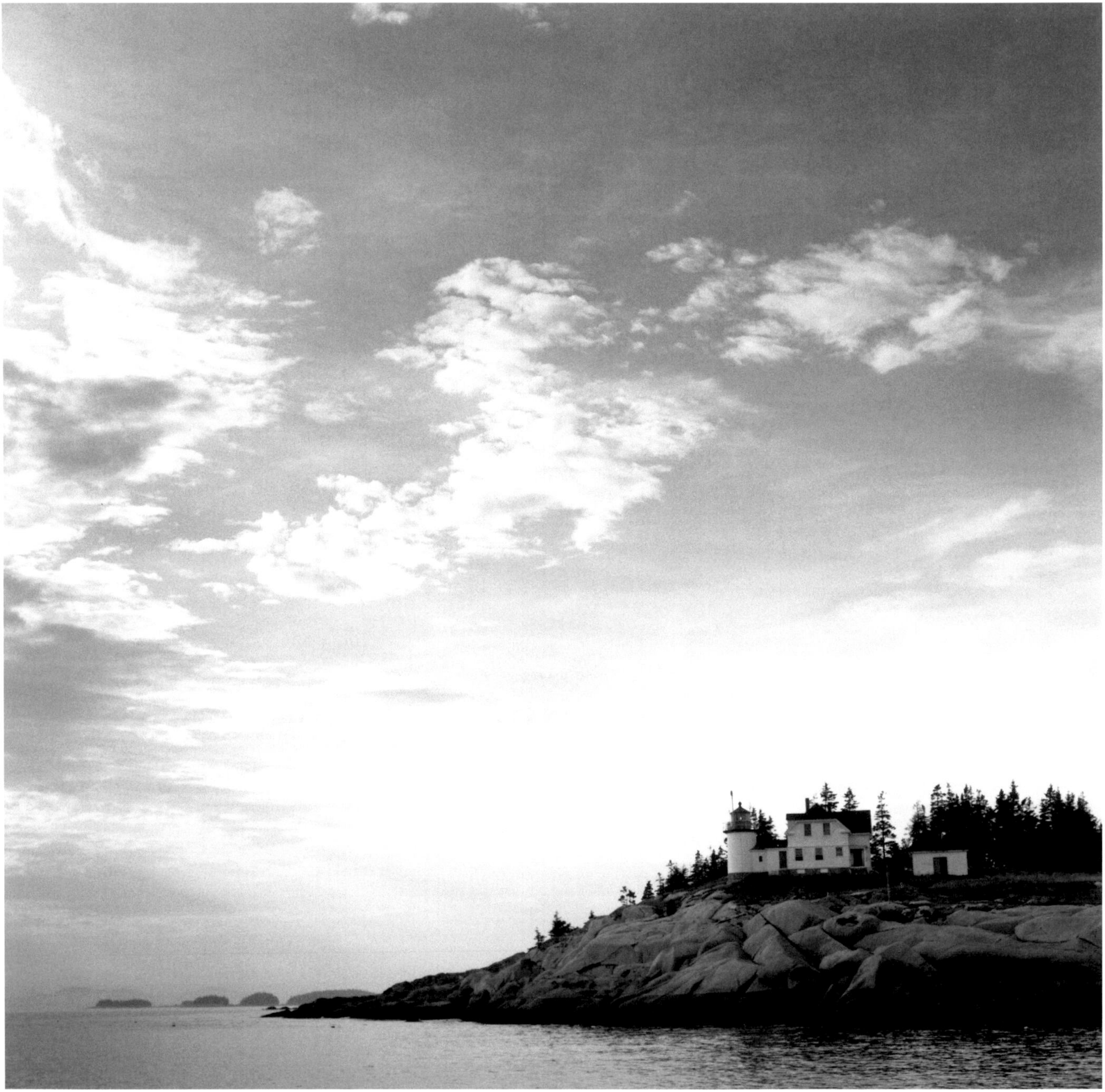

Camden, 1999

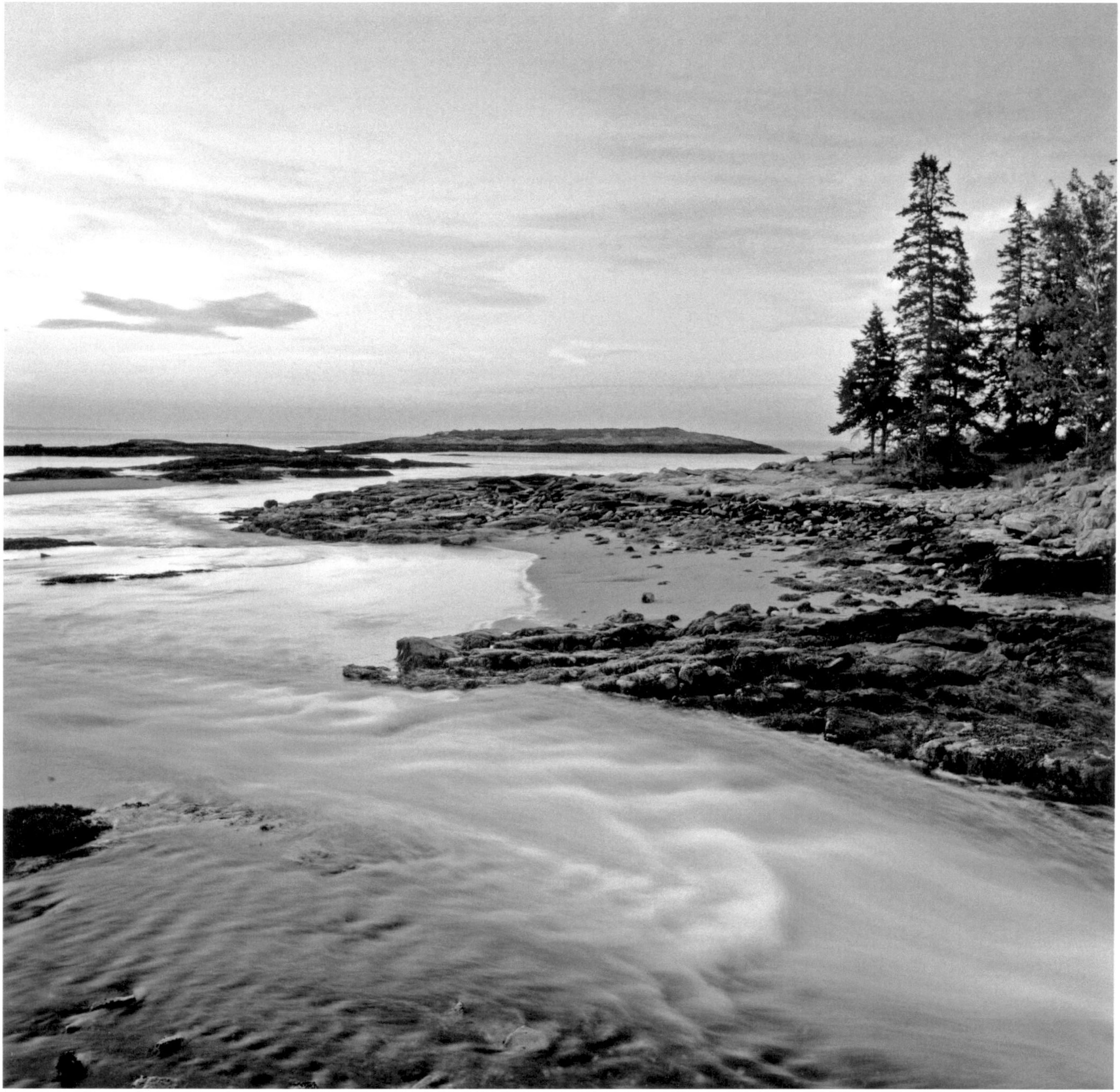

Reid State Park, 2002

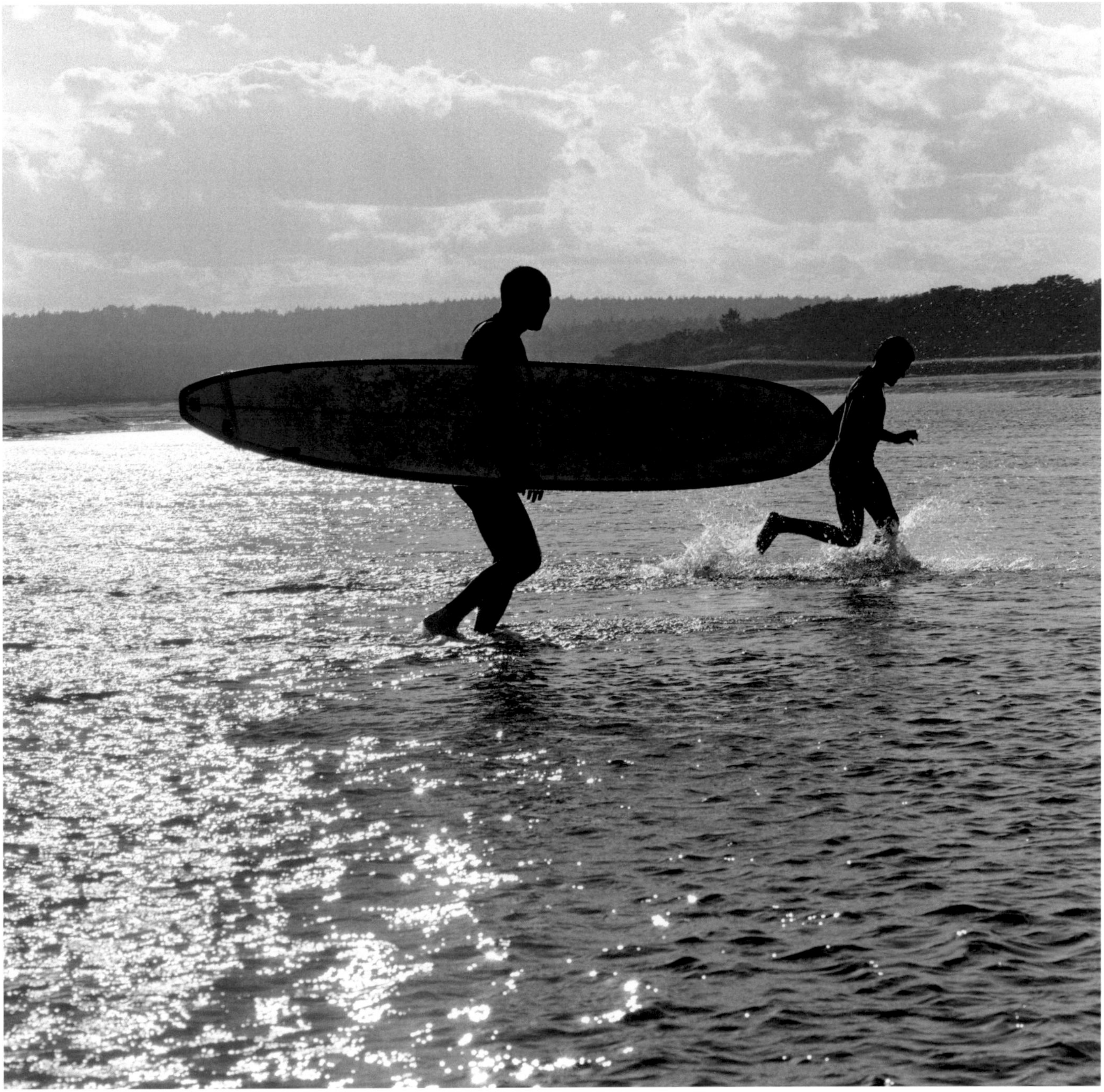

Popham Beach, 2006

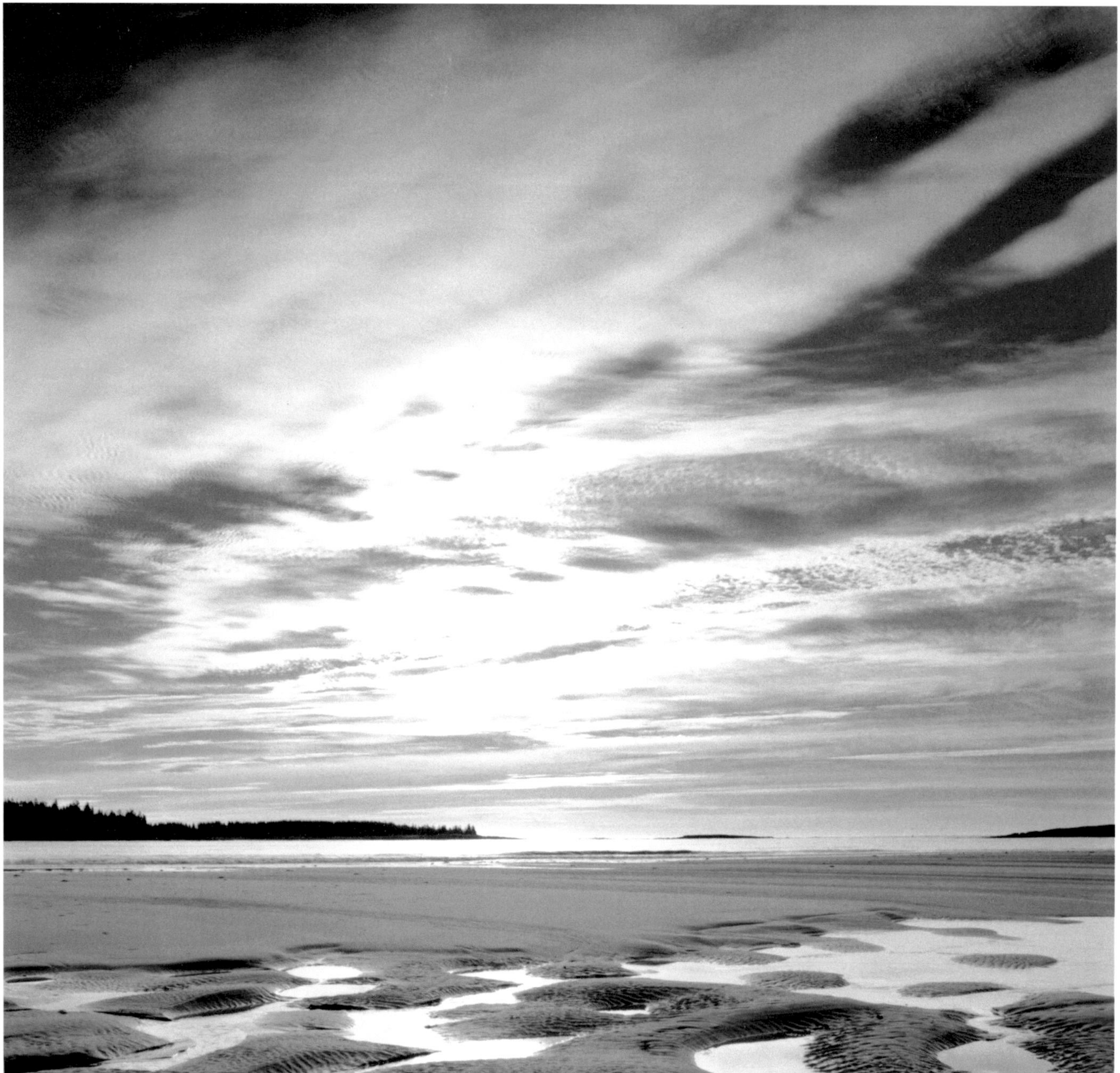
Popham Beach, 2011

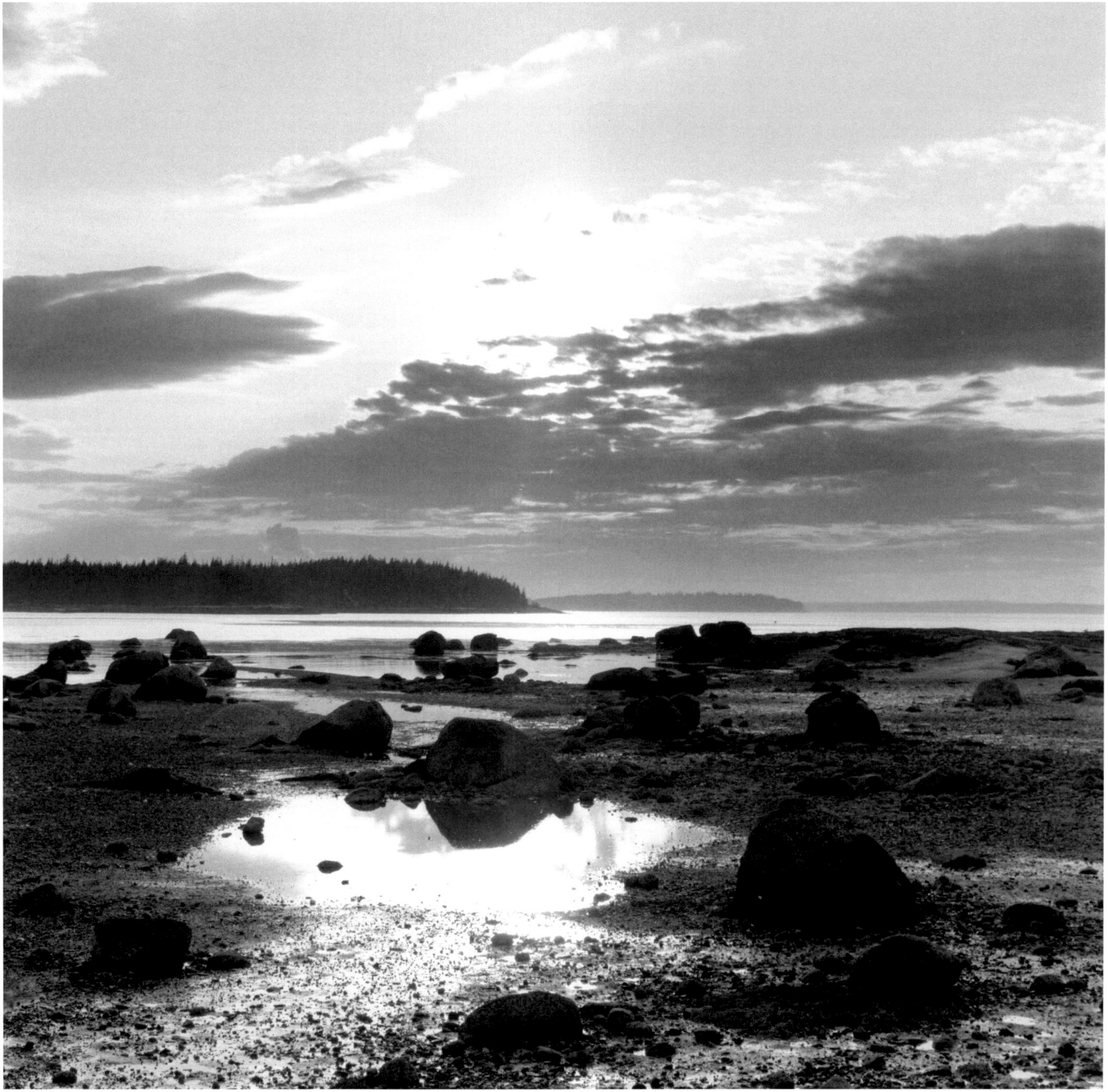
Naskeag, 2019

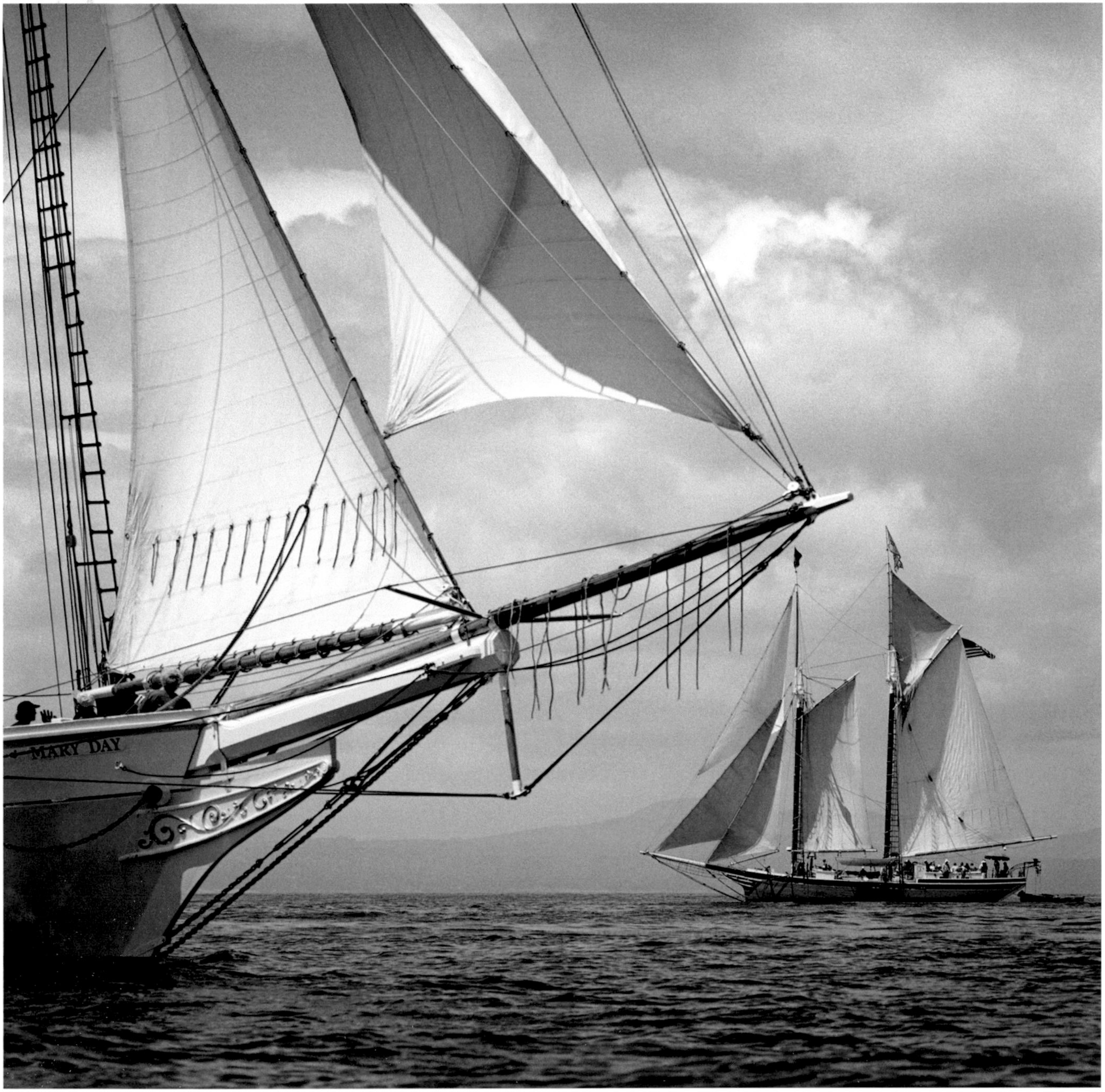

Rockland, 1998

Even in the vast and mysterious reaches of the sea
we are brought back to the fundamental truth
that nothing lives to itself.

—RACHEL CARSON

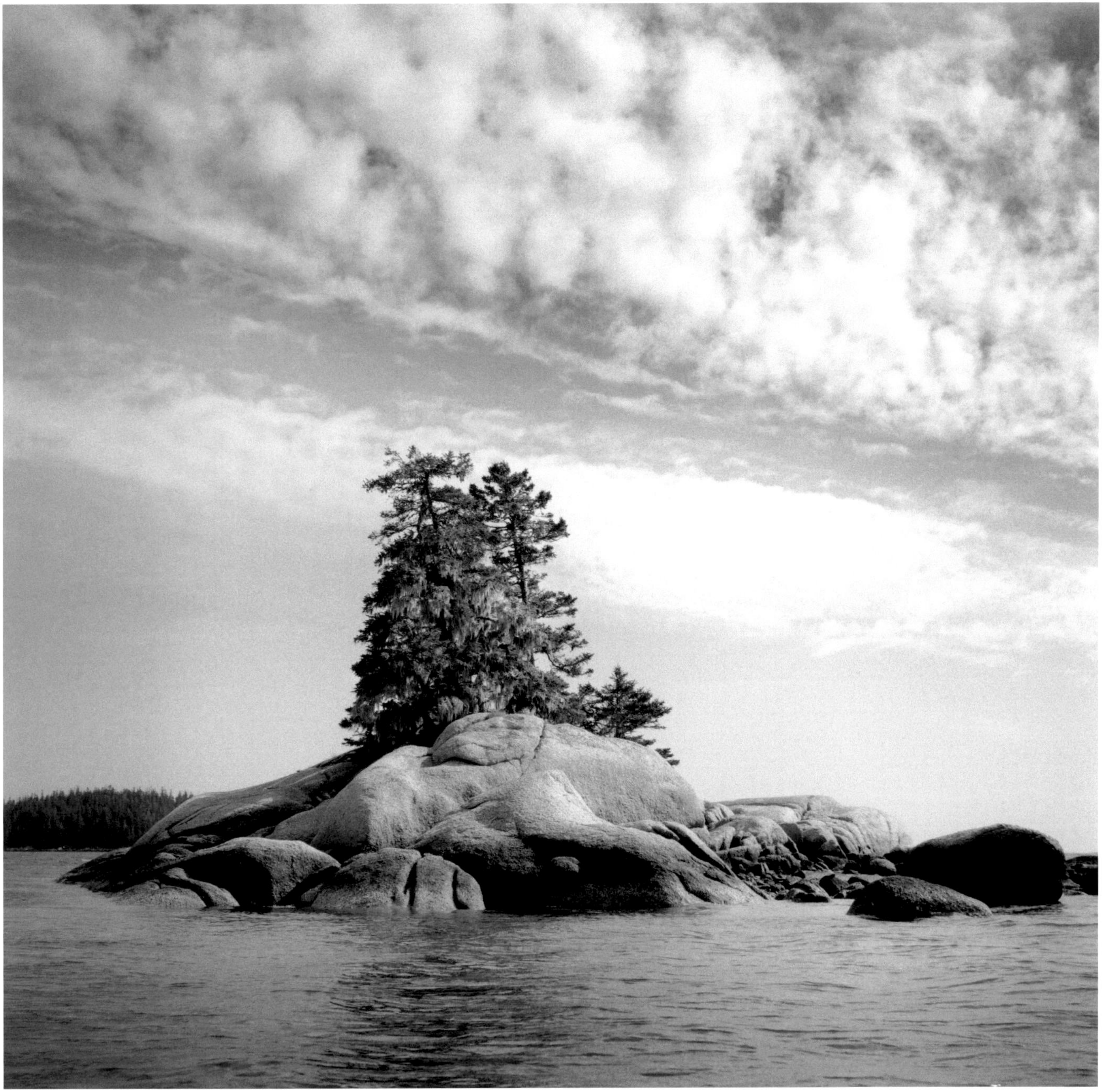

Babson Island, 2021

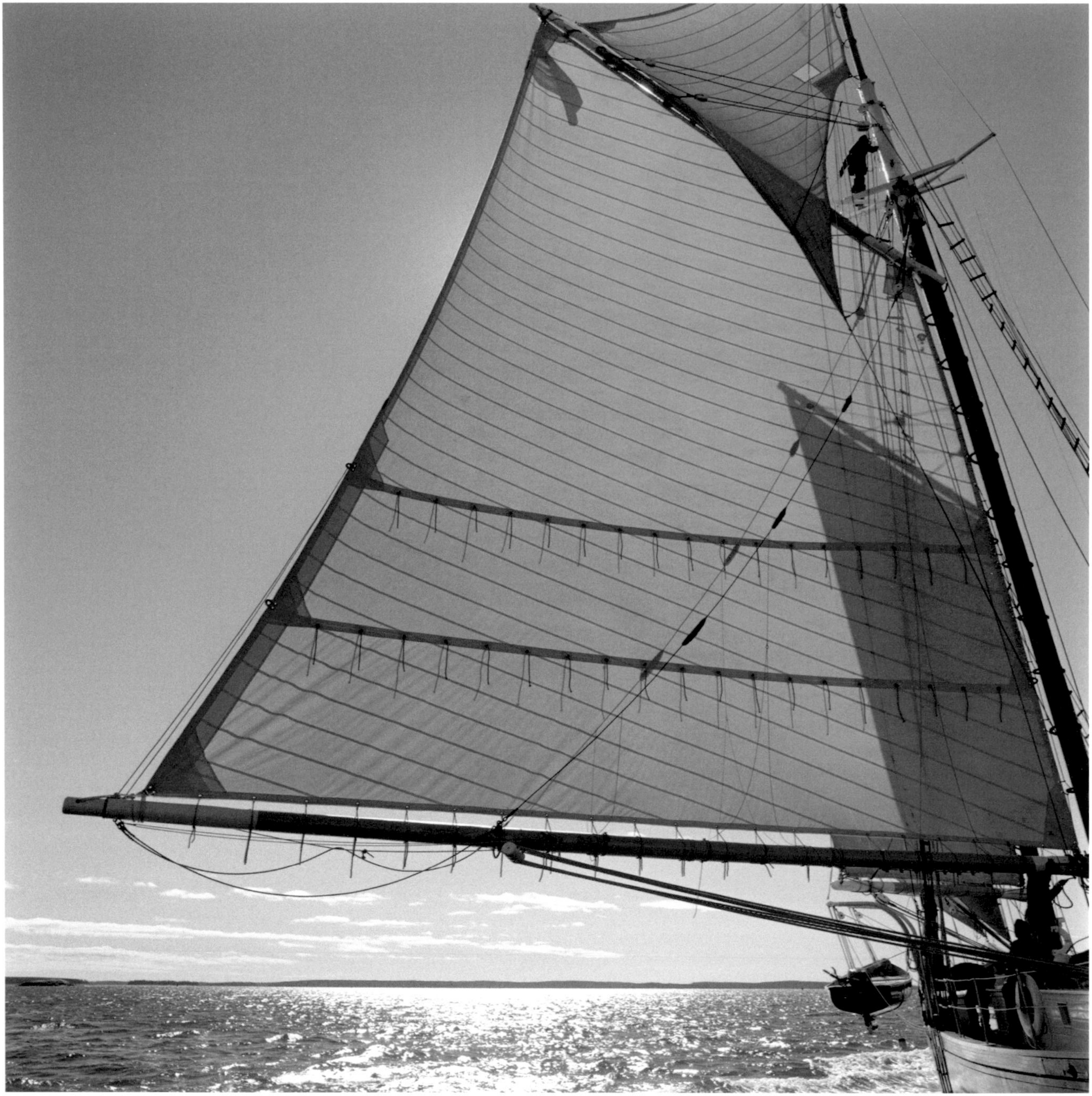
Eggemogin Reach, 2010

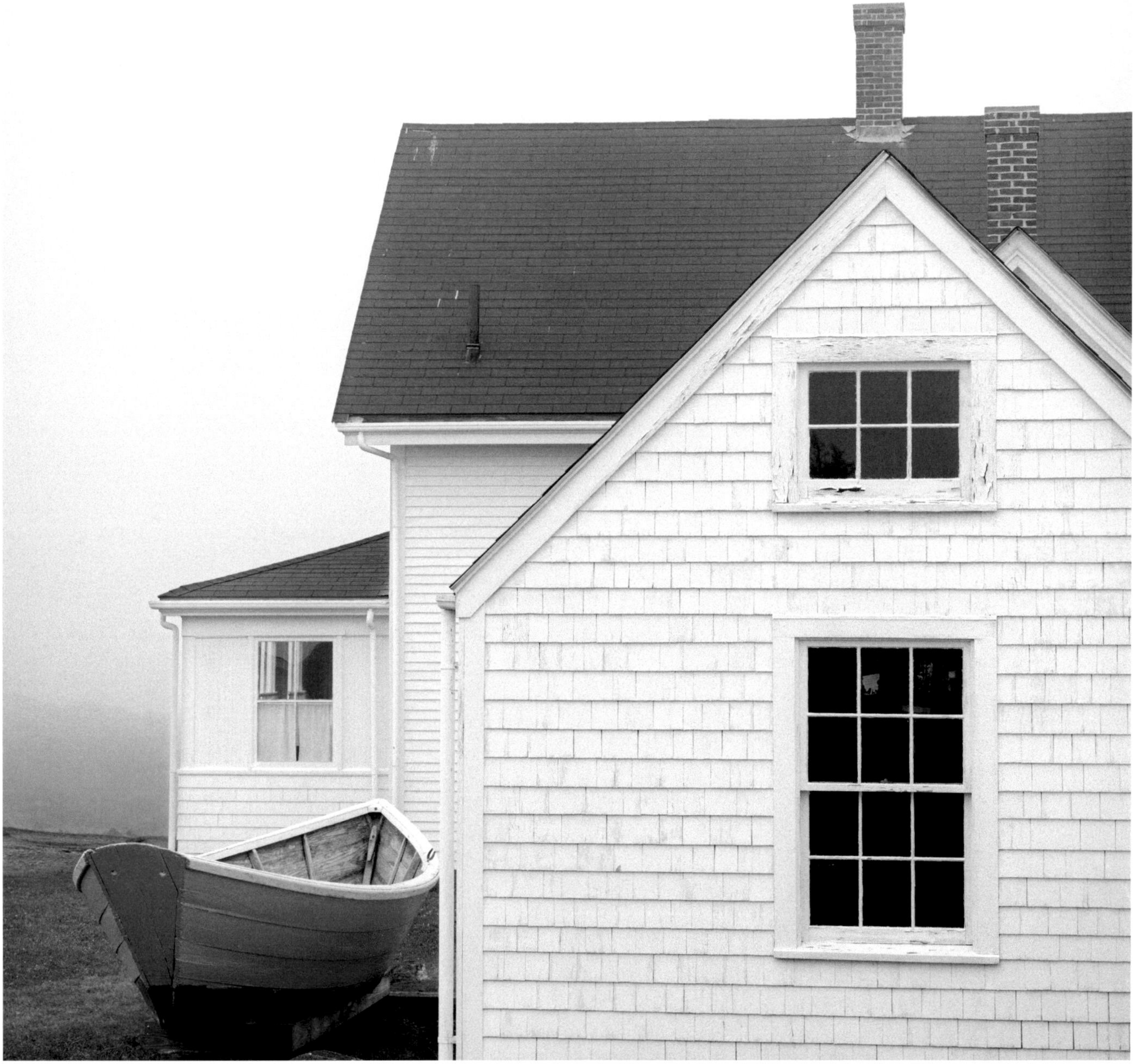

Monhegan Island, 2003

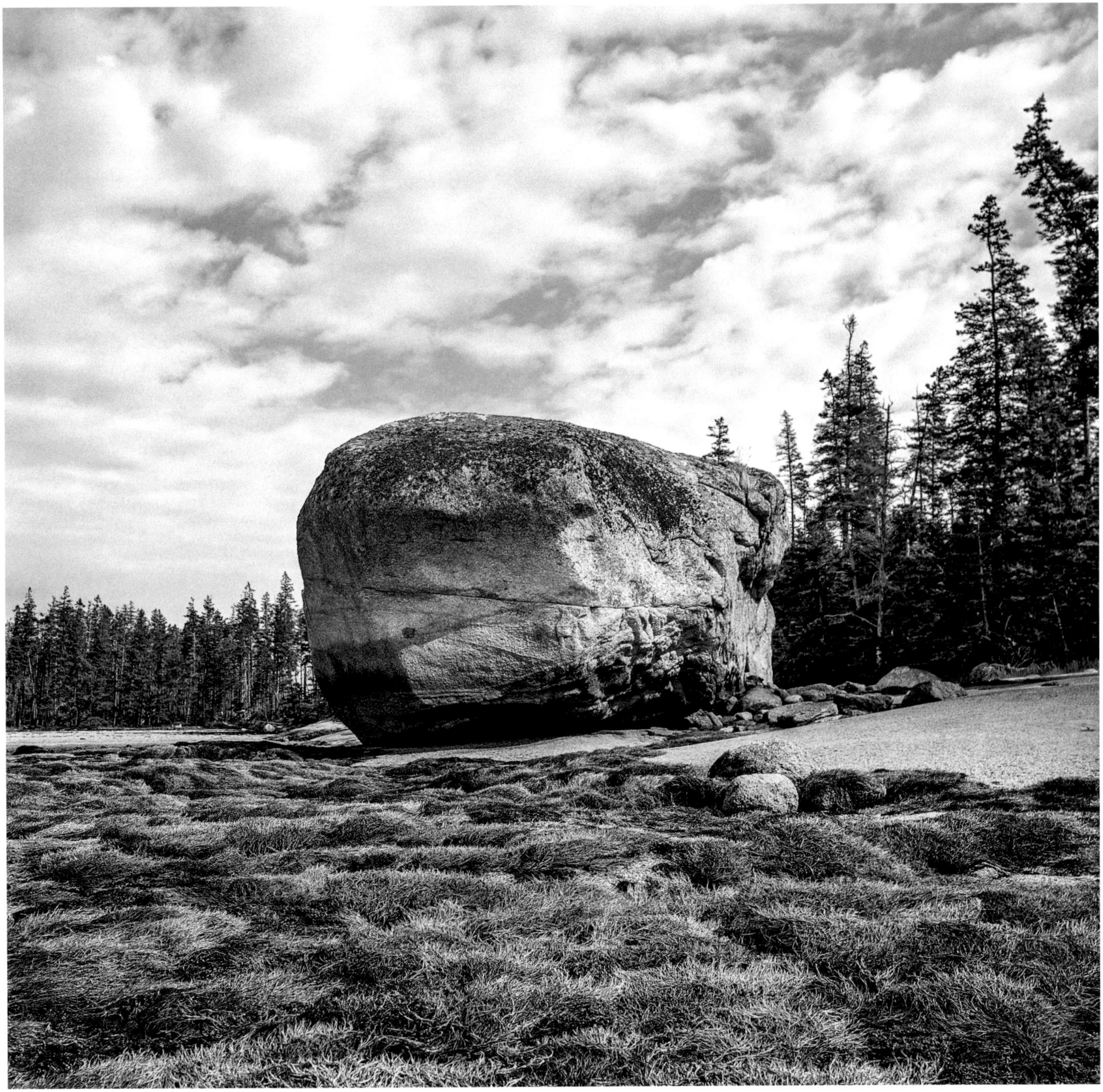

Hog Island, 2022

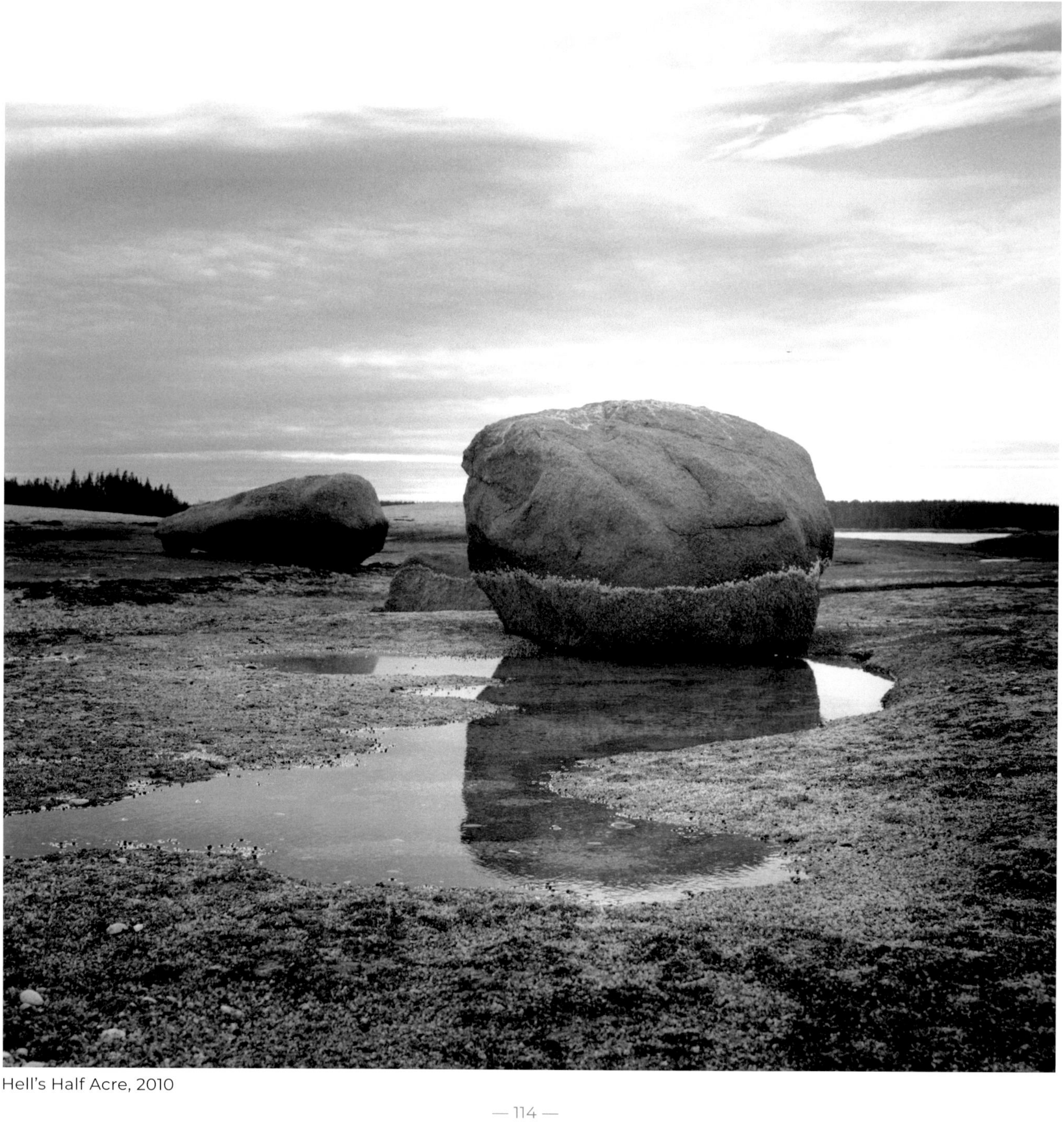

Hell's Half Acre, 2010

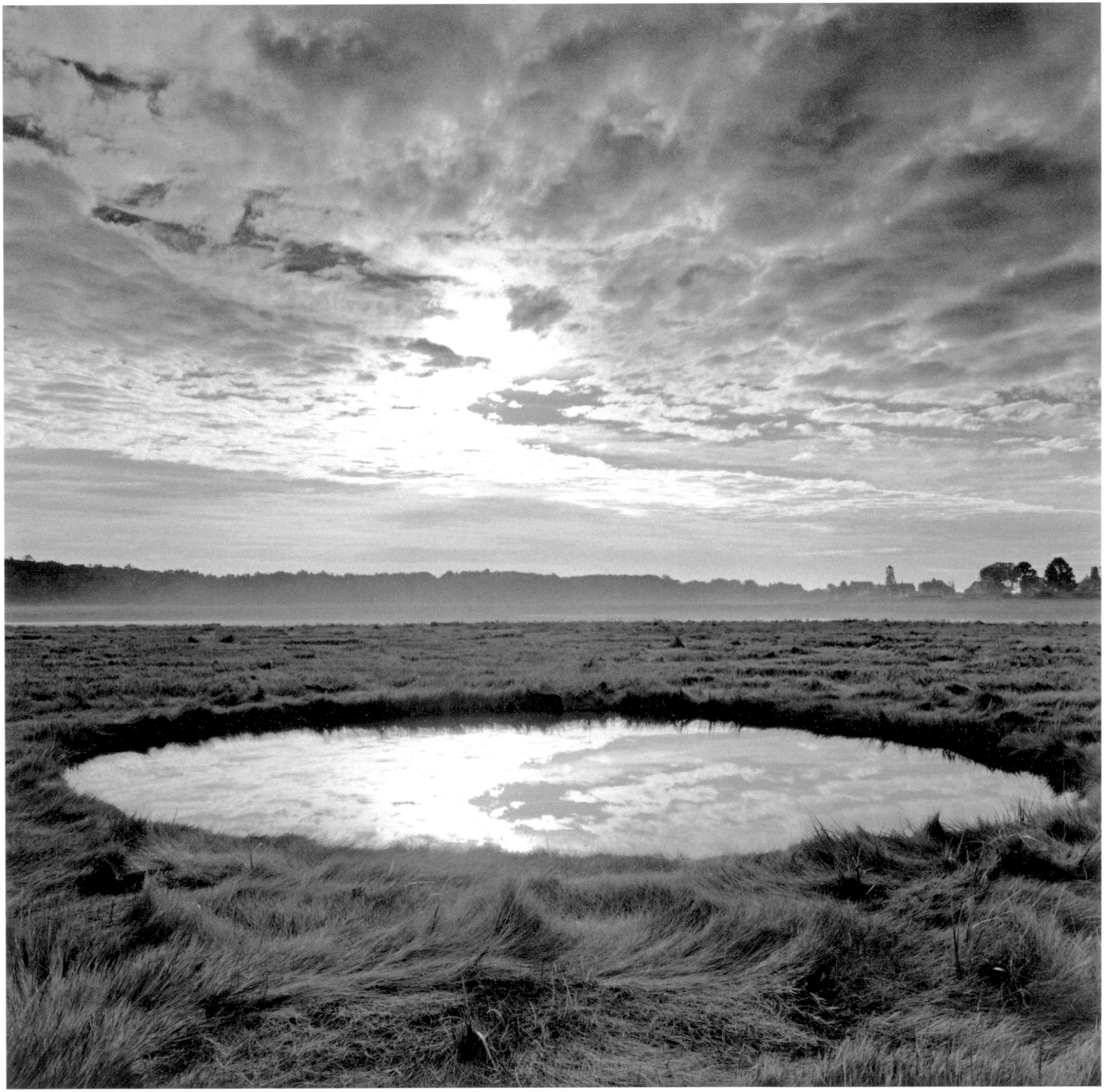

Parson's Beach, 2012

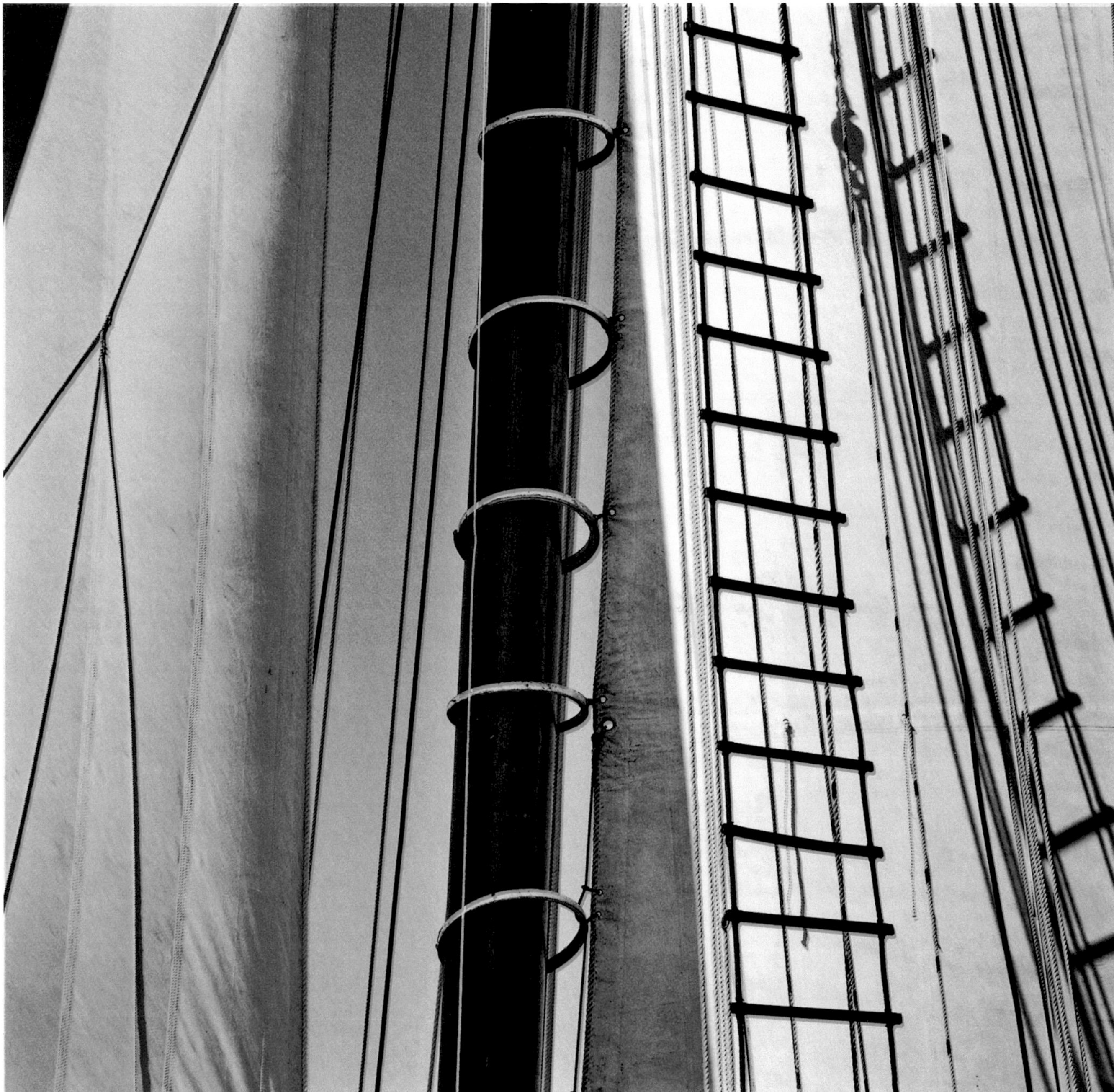

Rockland, 1998

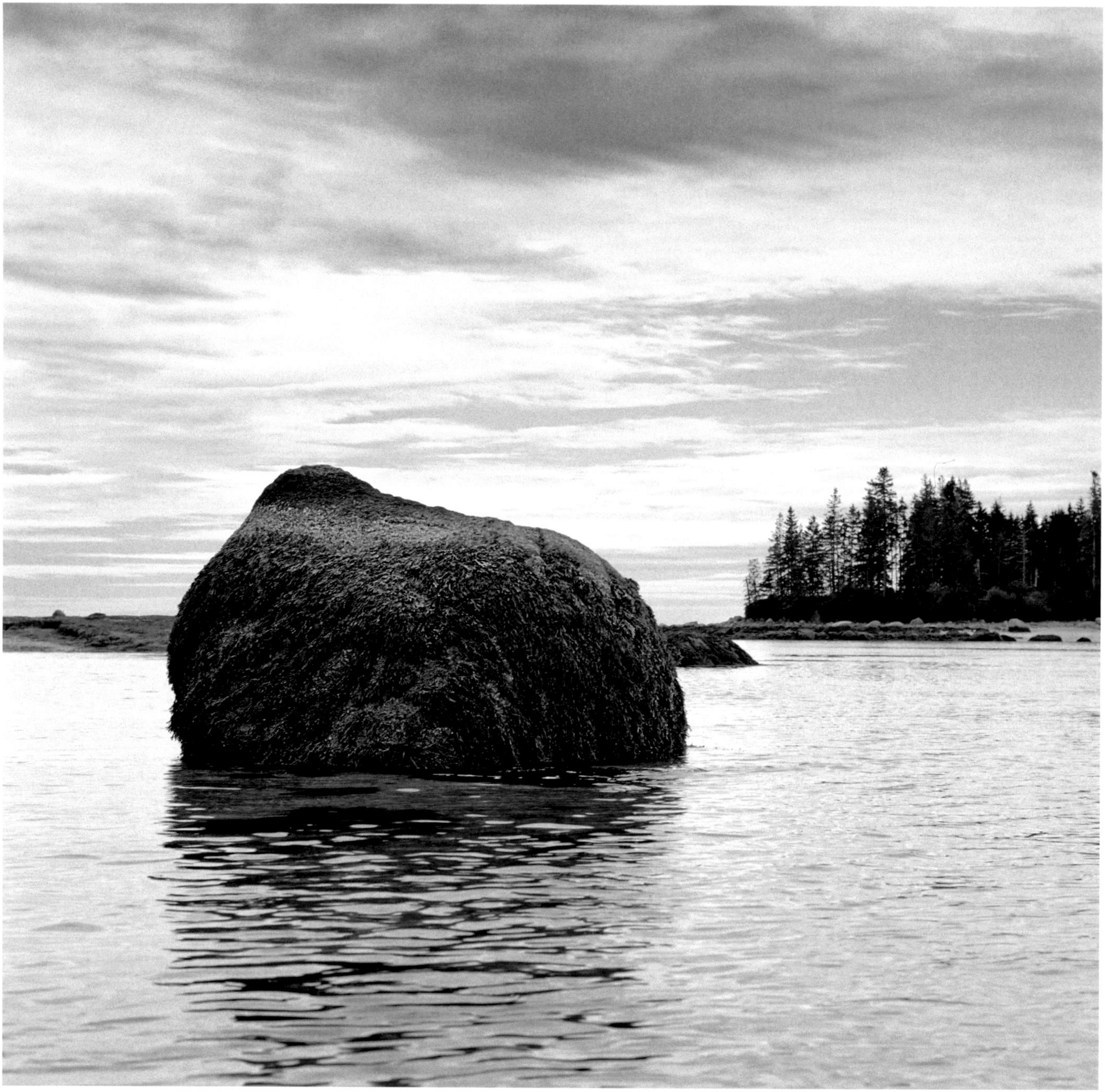
Naskeag Harbor, 2021

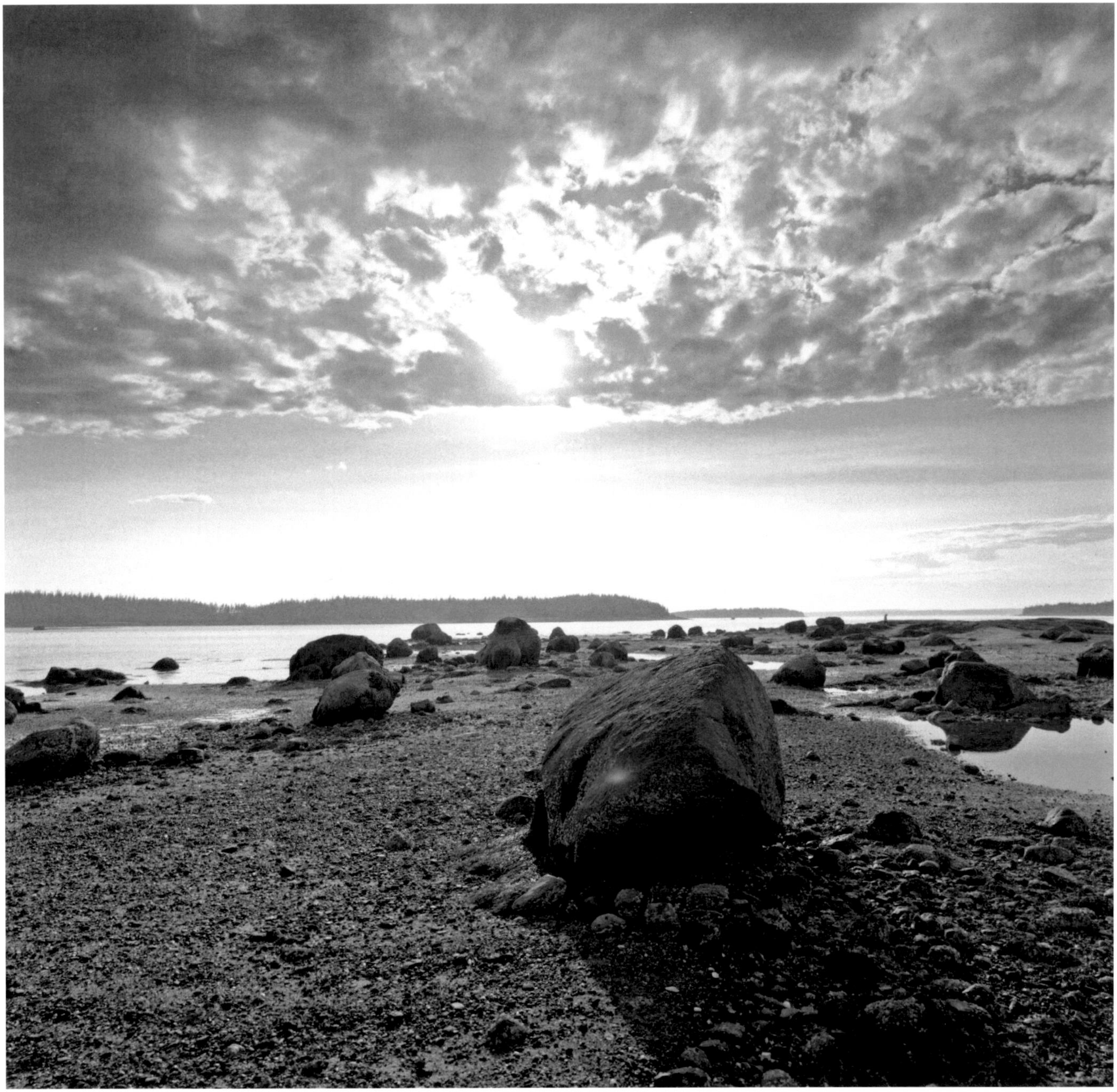

Naskeag Point, 2019

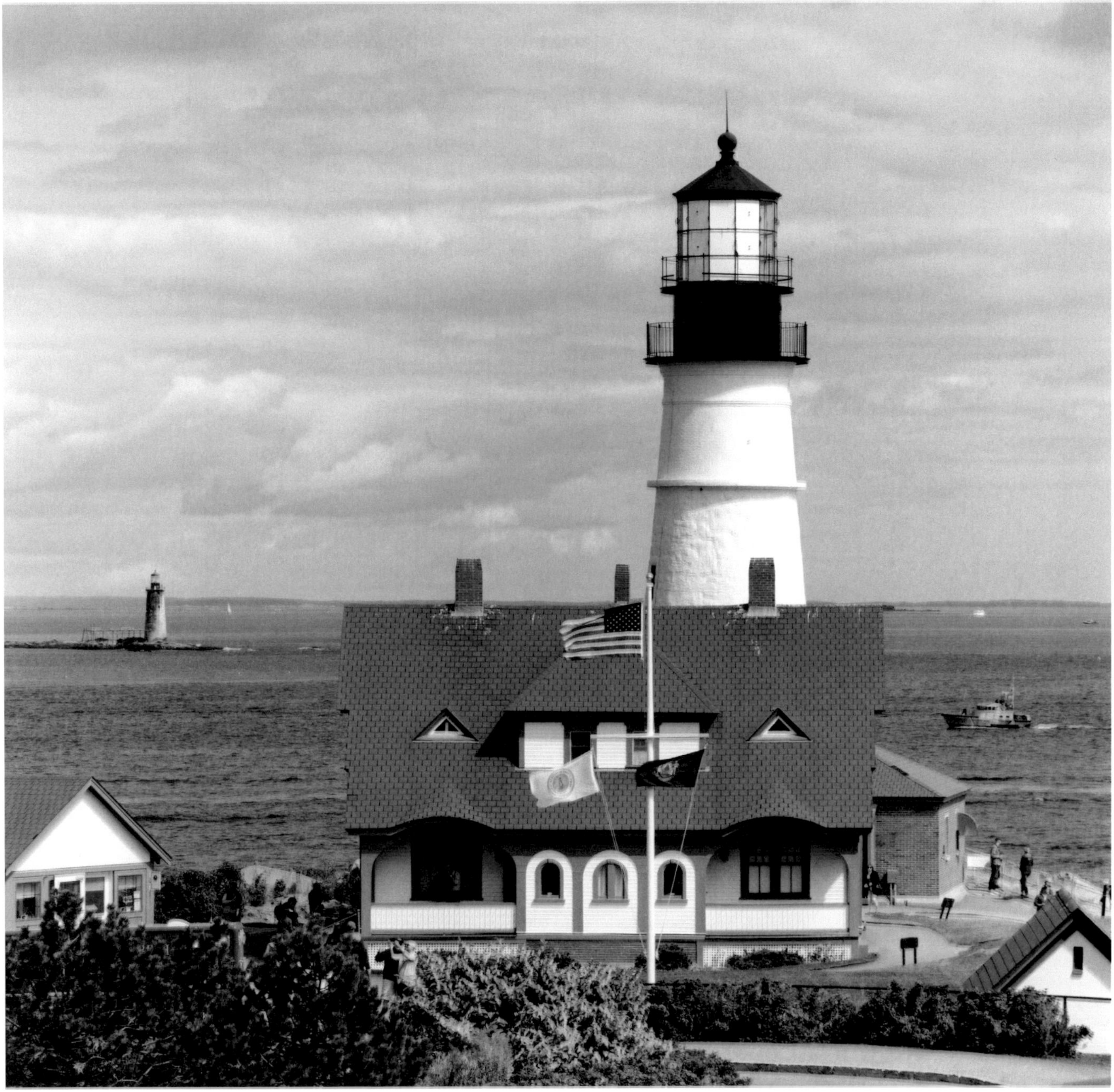

Portland Light, 2019

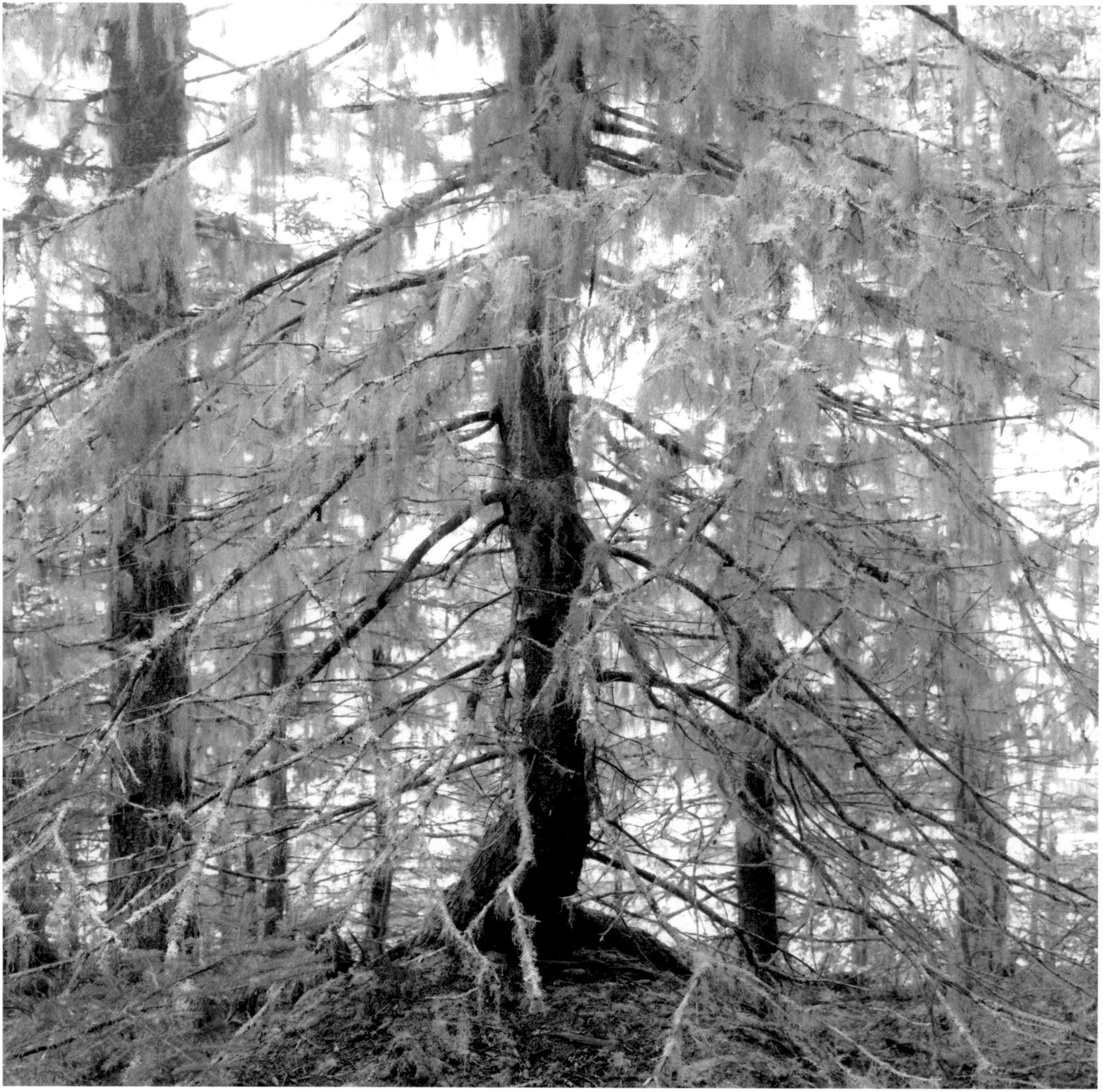

Spruce Tree Detail, 2021

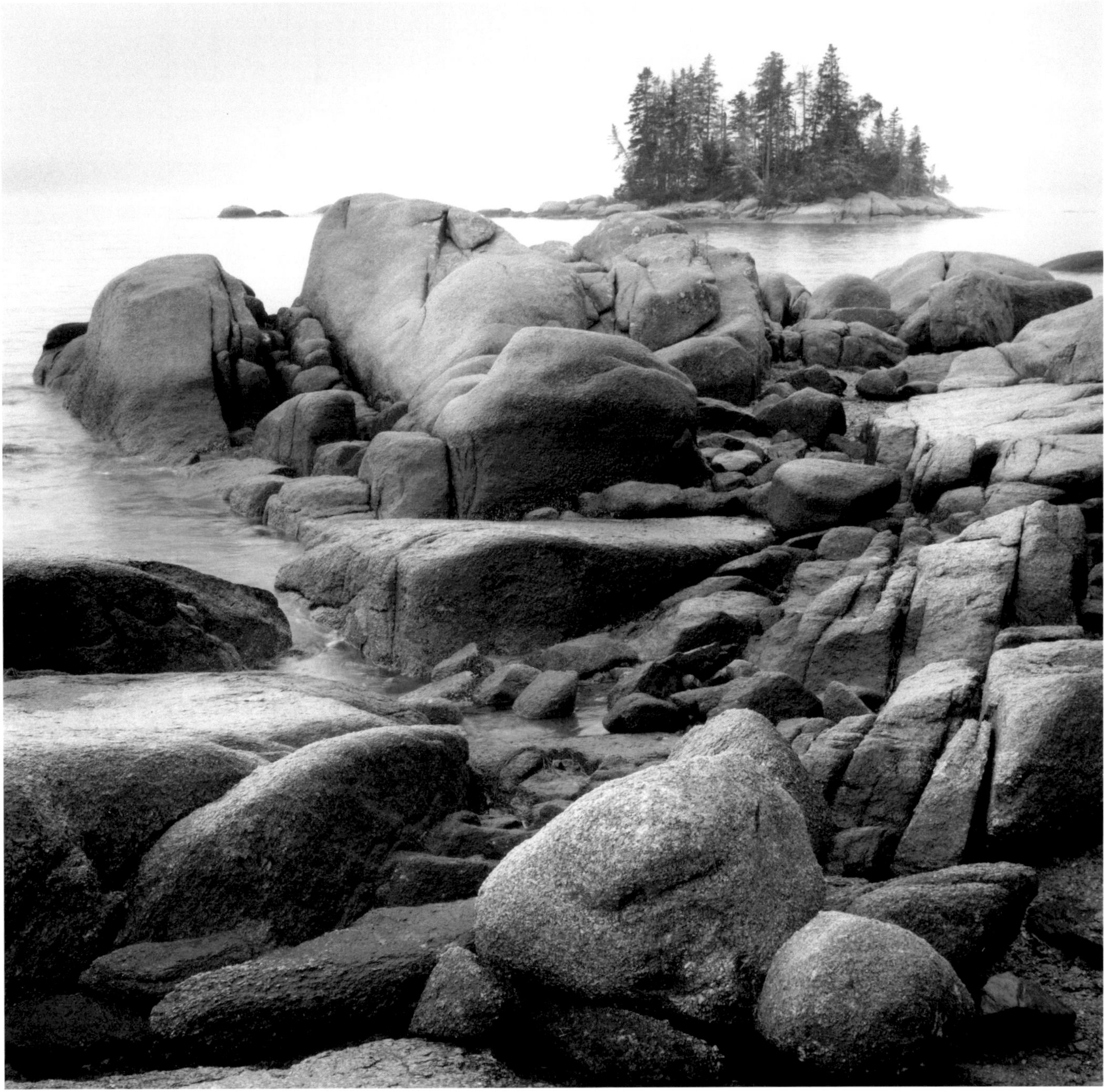

Sand Beach, 2023

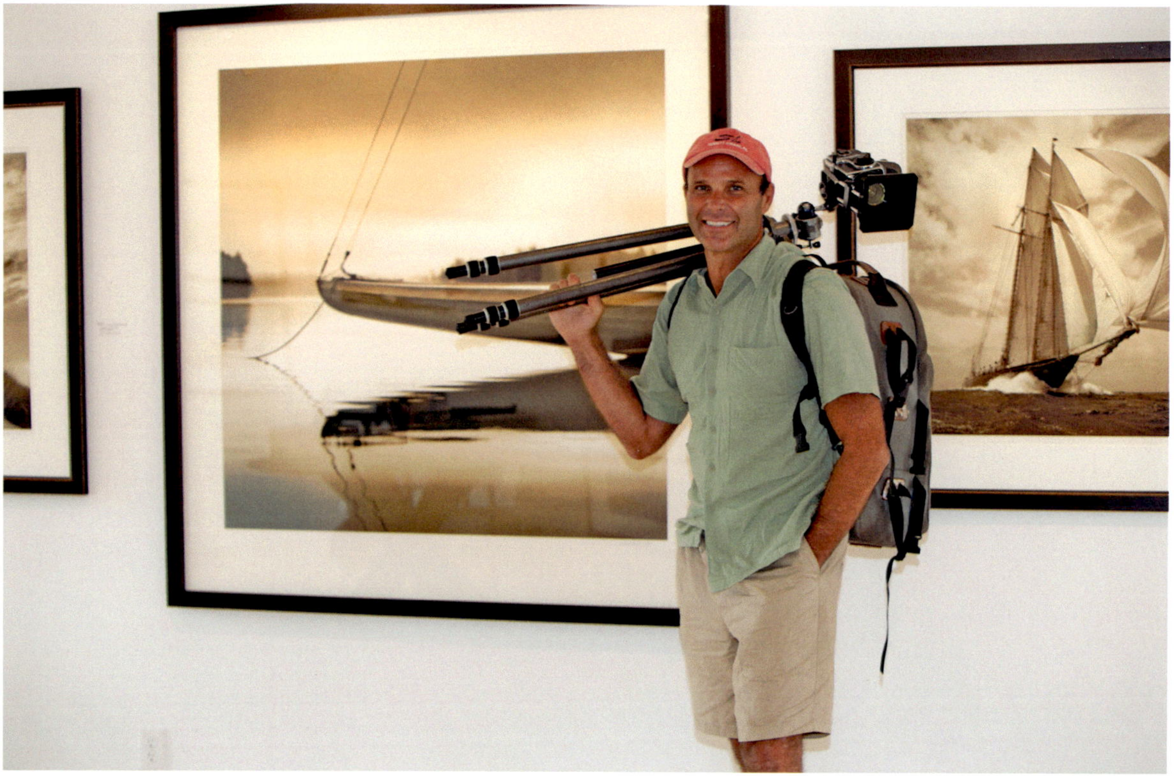

Photo Courtesy of Cindy Vallino, Focus Gallery, Chatham, MA

FOR MORE INFORMATION, PLEASE VISIT
WWW.MICHAELKAHN.COM

MICHAEL KAHN

Internationally renowned photographer Michael Kahn's stunning seascape and spectacular sailing photographs are exhibited in art galleries and museums throughout the world. With his 1950s camera, Michael travels extensively to photograph the world's finest boats and pristine seascapes. He collects his images on traditional black-and-white film and produces luminous silver gelatin prints in his darkroom. Michael's handmade photographs are warmly toned, signed, numbered in limited editions, and finished to museum standards. His traditional technique united with his distinctive sense of form, vision, and composition has helped him to be one of the most memorable photographers of our time.

Library of Congress Control Number: 2024931547

Creative design and input by Christine Yurick
Type set in Montserrat/Playfair Display

ISBN: 978-0-7643-6811-0
Printed in China

Published by Schiffer Publishing, Ltd.
4880 Lower Valley Road
Atglen, PA 19310
Phone: (610) 593-1777; Fax: (610) 593-2002
Email: info@schifferbooks.com
Web: www.schifferbooks.com

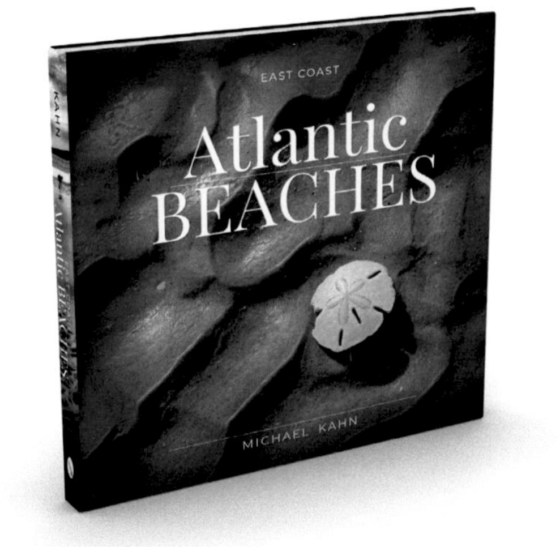

Other Schiffer Books by the Author:

East Coast Atlantic Beaches
ISBN: 978-0-7643-5931-6

Martha's Vineyard
ISBN: 978-0-7643-6269-9

Sailboats
ISBN: 978-0-7643-5930-9

The Healing Power of Water
ISBN: 978-0-7643-6265-1